"十二五"普通高等教育本科国家级规划教材

第三版
THIRD EDITION

NEW HORIZON COLLEGE ENGLISH
新视野大学英语 2

总主编：郑树棠

主 编：郑树棠　盈 文

编 者：郑树棠　盈 文　董美英　汪东萍
马 琴　郭遂红　苏 鹏

听说教程 LISTENING AND SPEAKING

智慧版

外语教学与研究出版社
FOREIGN LANGUAGE TEACHING AND RESEARCH PRESS
北京 BEIJING

图书在版编目（CIP）数据

新视野大学英语（第三版）听说教程 ：智慧版．2 ／郑树棠等主编 ；郑树棠等编．-- 北京 ：外语教学与研究出版社，2017.5（2024.1 重印）
（新视野大学英语 ：第三版 ／郑树棠总主编）
ISBN 978-7-5135-9018-1

Ⅰ．①新… Ⅱ．①郑… Ⅲ．①英语－听说教学－高等学校－教材 Ⅳ．①H319.9

中国版本图书馆 CIP 数据核字（2017）第 124717 号

出 版 人　王　芳
项目负责　高阿敏
责任编辑　徐　洋
责任校对　毕海英
封面设计　袁　凌
版式设计　涂　俐
出版发行　外语教学与研究出版社
社　　址　北京市西三环北路 19 号（100089）
网　　址　https://www.fltrp.com
印　　刷　北京市鑫霸印务有限公司
开　　本　889×1194　1/16
印　　张　8
版　　次　2017 年 7 月第 1 版　2024 年 1 月第 32 次印刷
书　　号　ISBN 978-7-5135-9018-1
定　　价　53.00 元（含 CD-ROM 光盘一张）

如有图书采购需求，图书内容或印刷装订等问题，侵权、盗版书籍等线索，请拨打以下电话或关注官方服务号：
客服电话：400 898 7008
官方服务号：微信搜索并关注公众号"外研社官方服务号"
外研社购书网址：https://fltrp.tmall.com

物料号：290180101

记载人类文明
沟通世界文化
www.fltrp.com

前言

1 编写背景

《新视野大学英语》于2001年首次出版，是一套教学理念独到、教学模式创新的立体化大学英语教材，自出版以来，受到高校师生的广泛好评。其所引领的将计算机网络技术引入大学英语教学的模式取得了显著的教学效果。2008年出版的《新视野大学英语》(第二版)在传承第一版经典特色的基础上，根据我国高等教育发展形势与教学改革趋势，对教学理念、教学内容和教学方法进行了全方位提升和完善。

外语教学始终同国家的发展息息相关。目前，我国的经济发展进入新常态，更加突出体现在重视质量、效益和可持续发展，以实现“两个一百年”的奋斗目标。国家的发展对于高素质国际化人才的需求，远远超过以往任何一个时期。即将颁布的《大学英语教学指南》根据国家发展和教学改革的需要，更加强调教学质量的重要性，强调对学生英语应用能力和综合文化素养的培养。根据《大学英语教学指南》，大学英语教学的主要内容可分为通用英语、专门用途英语和跨文化交际三个部分，由此形成相应的三大类课程。大学英语课程由必修课、限定选修课和任意选修课组成。

《新视野大学英语》（第三版）是为通用英语阶段设计的系列教材。编写团队本着严谨、务实的态度，深入调研高校大学英语课程教学现状，全面摸底大学新生入学英语水平，全面设计、全新编写了《新视野大学英语》(第三版)系列教材。第三版保持《新视野大学英语》一、二版的优势与特色，进一步落实教学分类指导、因材施教的原则，支持各高校根据学生入校英语水平，以及所选择专业的英语要求，适当调整通用英语阶段教学要求。

2 编写依据

《新视野大学英语》（第三版）认真贯彻《国家中长期教育改革和发展规划纲要（2010-2020）》和《关于全面提高高等教育质量的若干意见》的精神，在立足大学英语教学实际的基础上，引入先进外语教学理念，融合国际优质教育资源，采用科学的教学设计和多样的教学手段，有效提升学生英语综合应用能力，支持教师提高课堂教学质量，推动大学英语教学迈向新台阶。

《新视野大学英语》（第三版）在设计与编写中遵循以下整体原则：

在课程性质上体现工具性与人文性的有机结合

《新视野大学英语》（第三版）一方面遵循通用英语阶段语言学习规律，采取有效教学方法，全面提升学生的英语实际应用能力，一方面通过学习材料和活动设计培养学生的人文素养与综合素质，使学生在认识世界、了解社会、发现自我的过程中，树立正确的价值观，增进文化理解力，提高跨文化交际能力，从而实现工具性和人文性的有机统一。

在教学目标上体现个性化教学的需求

《新视野大学英语》（第三版）针对大学英语课程体系中通用英语课程的教学要求开发，总体目标是培养学生英语听、说、读、写、译的语言技能，同时达到增加知识、拓展视野、提高能力、提升文化素养的目的。教材共有4个级别，在主题内容、词汇分布和练习形式等方面充分考虑了难度的递进，学校可以根据学生的起点水平进行个性化选择，使学生通过不同级别的学习达到通用英语阶段的基本要求或提高要求。

在教学理念上体现“以教师为主导、以学生为主体”

《新视野大学英语》（第三版）体现“以教师为主导、以学生为主体”的教学理念，采用丰富多样的练习设计，激发学生学习兴趣，便于教师灵活指导，选取最佳的教学方法，鼓励学生主动参与，提高课堂教学效果。此外，教材注重培养学生的学习能力和学习策略，通过探究式、合作式活动引导学生积极思考和创新实践，通过对新知识、文化点和学习策略的讲解帮助学生掌握正确方法，使教学活动真正实现由“教”向“学”的转变。

在教学手段上体现教学的立体化、个性化与便捷性

《新视野大学英语》（第三版）充分体现信息技术给教育模式带来的变革，根据学生学习特点、教师教学习惯和学校教学环境的变化，构建U校园智慧教学云平台，为教、学、评、测、研提供全方位支持，通过高效便捷的教学工具、丰富多样的教学资源与无缝对接的多终端支持，助力教师优化教学流程、丰富教学设计、创新教学模式；同时，满足学生在多模态环境下的个性化学习，帮助师生共建智慧课堂，实现智慧学习。

3 教材特色

《新视野大学英语》（第三版）的筹划、设计和编写历经多年，编写团队本着对教学负责、对学生负责的态度，精心选材，严谨编写，力求在帮助学生切实提高语言交际能力的同时，还能引导他们辨别多元视角、对比不同文化、深入思考问题，有助于他们成为具有社会责任感、国际视野和创新精神的高素质人才。《新视野大学英语》（第三版）的教材特色主要体现在以下方面：

选材富有时代气息，体现思辨性和人文性

教材充分考虑时代发展和新一代大学生的特点，选材富有时代气息，主题多样，涵盖社会、历史、经济、哲学、科技、文化等不同领域。选篇注重思想性和趣味性的结合，文章安排注意观点的相互碰撞和补充，激发学生的思辨力与创新思维，培养学生以多元视角看待个人、社会和世界。视听说分册包含丰富的BBC原版音视频，语言鲜活、语音纯正、语境真实，展现各国风土人情和文化传统，开拓学生视野，增强学生的文化感知力和理解力。

练习活动形式多样，培养语言能力和跨文化能力

与一、二版相比，第三版教材保持了练习的丰富性和系统性，并进一步加强了练习的思辨性、应用性和文化对比性。练习设计遵循语言学习的内在规律，目的明确、安排有序，既包括单项技能训练，也包括综合语言运用，输入与输出结合，线下与线上结合。语言活动注重思维训练，培养跨文化意识，通过批判性问题启迪学生思考，通过对比翻译引导学生理解和表达中西文化差异，通过场景真实的交际任务培养学生解决实际问题的能力。

教学设计循序渐进，打好基础，学用结合

教材设计基于对大学生英语水平和高校英语教学现状的细致调研，编写时充分考虑基础教育阶段与高等教育阶段英语教学的衔接，各级别定位清晰，难度逐步提升。教材通过科学严谨的材料选择与词汇编制，对核心词汇及搭配的重点练习，以及对语言技能的综合训练，帮助学生进一步打好语言基本功。同时，教材注意语言知识与语言应用的关系，通过练习引导学生掌握规律、举一反三、活用语言，提高语言的实际应用能力。

教学资源丰富立体，引领混合式教学模式

第三版教材倡导课堂教学与自主学习结合的混合式教学模式，通过创建全新的U校园智慧教学云平台，提供丰富的教学资源、立体的教学环境和便捷的多终端教学管理工具，整合混合式教学全流程，帮助教师实现课堂内外的有机结合与开放互动。除主干课程外，在数字课程体系中新增配套类课程（如第三版系列内的“长篇阅读”和“综合训练”等）和拓展类课程（如技能提升课程、语言文化课程、商务职场课程等），院校可自主选择线下、线上或混合教学的模式。教材同时配备PC端和移动端数字课程，优化教学体验，提升教学效果。此外，外研随身学App等移动学习工具帮助学生充分利用碎片化时间，向主动学习、自主学习、个性化学习的方向发展。

教学与评估并重，帮助教师实现教学相长

第三版教材为教师提供丰富多样的数字化教学资源，便于教师进行个性化教学，还创建了教师实时共建和分享备课资源的Ucreate交流平台，鼓励教师合作创新。同时，教材提供全面的形成性与终结性评测手段，多维度、可视化的学习数据统计以及基于数据的学情预测和教学建议，便于教师及时、准确了解学生学习状况，调整教学思路，改进教学方法。此外，对基于数字技术的混合式教学模式、网上合作学习模式、教学评估模式等新领域的探索，还能为教师提供研究思路与实证数据，助益教师的教学与学术发展。

4 教材构成

《新视野大学英语》（第三版）根据通用英语阶段的基本要求或提高要求，设计有1—4级，供两个学年使用。每一级别包含《读写教程》（配教师用书）、《听说教程》（配教师用书）、《视听说教程》（配教师用书）、《泛读教程》、《长篇阅读》和《综合训练》。同时提供与教材配套的学习光盘、教学课件、试题库、U校园智慧教学云平台、移动应用等教学资源。不同课程、不同媒体之间紧密联系，相互支持，互为补充。

《新视野大学英语》（第三版）系列教材均为全新编写。《听说教程》配合《读写教程》的中心话题展开多种形式的听说训练。《泛读教程》、《长篇阅读》和《综合训练》三个分册也与《读写教程》单元主题呼应，是对《读写教程》的补充、强化与拓展。《视听说教程》基于英国培生教育出版集团的经典教材*Speakout*进行全面改编，既保留了视听资源地道鲜活的优势，又符合国内高校教学的需求与特点。

《读写教程》以有效巩固和扎实培养学生的语言知识和技能为特色，通过视角多元、内涵丰富的选篇以及形式多样的练习，着重提高学生的读、写、译能力。《听说教程》听力素材形式多样，内容生动丰富，设计循序渐进，帮助学生夯实语言基础，切实提升英语听说交流能力。《视听说教程》视听资源生动地道，文化信息丰富，交际场景真实，有效提高学生的听说能力与跨文化交际能力。《泛读教程》注重阅读方法培养，提供多样的选篇和练习，帮助学生扩展词汇、开阔视野，提高英语阅读能力。《长篇阅读》通过有效的训练，培养学生的阅读策略，提高"快速 + 准确"获取信息的能力。《综合训练》与《读写教程》紧密相联，提供词汇、语法、翻译和阅读等方面的练习，帮助学生巩固语言知识，提高语言技能。

《新视野大学英语》（第三版）遵循分类指导、因材施教的教学原则，通过多种途径为个性化教学提供支持。系列教材中包括不同级别和不同分册，还提供丰富多样的网络课程与数字化教学资源，为教学提供了较大的选择空间。教师可根据学校和学生实际情况，依据基于本校特色的教学目标和教学要求，自主选择教学材料和教学方法，逐步提高学生的语言能力和跨文化交际能力，培养学生的自主学习能力和综合文化素养，从而实现相应的教学目标。

5 编写团队

《新视野大学英语》（第三版）项目总负责人、教材总主编为上海交通大学郑树棠教授。全国数十所高校的几十名资深教授和中青年骨干教师参与了系列教材的设计、编写和制作。参与《视听说教程》编写和制作的还有英国培生教育出版集团的英语教育专家和教材编写专家。在教材编写和修改定稿的过程中，有多位外籍专家学者参与审定和指导。

《新视野大学英语》（第三版）应新时代的召唤诞生，从筹划到出版历经数年，期待以全新面貌为新时期的大学英语教学发展贡献力量。因教材为全新编写，难免有不足之处，还将在使用过程中收集反馈建议，希望专家、老师和同学在审阅和使用中多提宝贵意见，以使教材不断改进和完善。

编 者

2015 年 3 月

编写及使用说明

《听说教程》是《新视野大学英语》（第三版）系列教材中的主干教材。本教程以《大学英语教学指南》的精神为指导，在素材选择和练习设计上充分考虑大学生目前的语言能力和认知水平，全面提高学生英语听说交流能力。

1 教材特色

听力素材内容丰富，体裁多样

听力素材与《读写教程》主题相呼应，但突破了《读写教程》主题限制，其内容覆盖面广，涉及校园生活、人际交往、求职就业、自然科技等话题，从而帮助学生开阔视野，提升素养；听力素材包含新闻报道、长对话、篇章、讲座等不同体裁，有针对性地提高学生的听力技能。

语言浅显，背景知识难度适中，着力提高听说技能

大量研究无可争辩地证明，听说教学应主要以常用词汇为主。《听说教程》不刻意扩大词汇量，听力素材以常用普通词汇为主体，《听说教程 1》和《听说教程 2》几乎没有生词，《听说教程 3》和《听说教程 4》出现的少量生词也是《读写教程》中已学过的词汇。素材中的语法也不一定要求完整，体现了听说教程的特点。《听说教程》注意避免英美文化、历史等内容在同一个短段落中密集出现，所出现的文化、历史等知识也是常见的，并在学生的认知范围内，避免人为增加因背景知识带来的难度。

内容循序渐进，难度梯度合理

合理控制听力素材的长度与难度，语言标准地道，语速循序渐进，难度逐级递增，每一单元的英、美音听力素材基本各占一半，男女声比例也基本平衡。口语活动设计科学、操作性强，从情景对话、小组讨论到口头汇报，活动难度逐级递增，以逐步提高学生的口语表达能力。

输入与输出有机结合，综合提高听说能力

从基础听力训练入手，有效引导学生掌握听力技能与策略和常用交际表达用语，实现输入与输出有机结合，帮助学生内化语言知识，积累语言的表达方式，实现听听说说，听说结合。口语活动始终围绕听力素材的内容展开，以帮助学生有效地表达个人观点，体现了听说结合、全面提升语言应用能力的特点。

教学资源立体，满足个性化需求

充分体现数字化时代特色，提供配套数字课程、移动应用、教学管理平台、多媒体光盘、试题库等教学资源，既能为教师提供强大教学支持，助力提升教学效果，同时也满足新一代学习者的个性化需求，培养自主学习能力。

2 单元结构

《听说教程 2》全书共 8 个单元，内容与《读写教程》相呼应，但突破了《读写教程》主题的限制。在课时条件允许的条件下，可以不受《读写教程》的教学进度限制。

《听说教程 2》的单元结构如下：

<table>
<tr><td colspan="3">Warm-up</td></tr>
<tr><td rowspan="2">Listening</td><td colspan="2">Understanding a conversation</td></tr>
<tr><td colspan="2">Understanding a passage</td></tr>
<tr><td rowspan="4">Speaking</td><td rowspan="2">Practicing conversational skills</td><td>Useful expressions</td></tr>
<tr><td>Model dialogues</td></tr>
<tr><td colspan="2">Listening and speaking: Conversation</td></tr>
<tr><td colspan="2">Listening and speaking: Passage</td></tr>
<tr><td colspan="3">Unit report</td></tr>
<tr><td rowspan="2">Homework</td><td colspan="2">Section A: Understanding news reports</td></tr>
<tr><td colspan="2">Section B: Understanding passages</td></tr>
</table>

各板块使用说明：

Warm-up

通过不同形式的听力活动，引入单元主题，激发学生兴趣；练习设置了“What did you hear?”和“How would you respond?”两个环节，启发学生挖掘信息，并开展讨论。

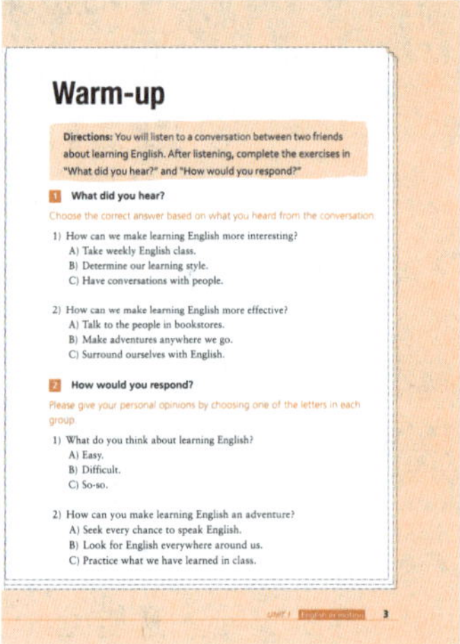

Warm-up

Directions: You will listen to a conversation between two friends about learning English. After listening, complete the exercises in "What did you hear?" and "How would you respond?"

1 What did you hear?

Choose the correct answer based on what you heard from the conversation.

1) How can we make learning English more interesting?
A) Take weekly English class.
B) Determine our learning style.
C) Have conversations with people.

2) How can we make learning English more effective?
A) Talk to the people in bookstores.
B) Make adventures anywhere we go.
C) Surround ourselves with English.

2 How would you respond?

Please give your personal opinions by choosing one of the letters in each group.

1) What do you think about learning English?
A) Easy.
B) Difficult.
C) So-so.

2) How can you make learning English an adventure?
A) Seek every chance to speak English.
B) Look for English everywhere around us.
C) Practice what we have learned in class.

3

Listening

每单元提供两段听力材料，包含长对话和篇章，选材长度与难度贴近学生语言水平，有针对性地训练听力技巧。

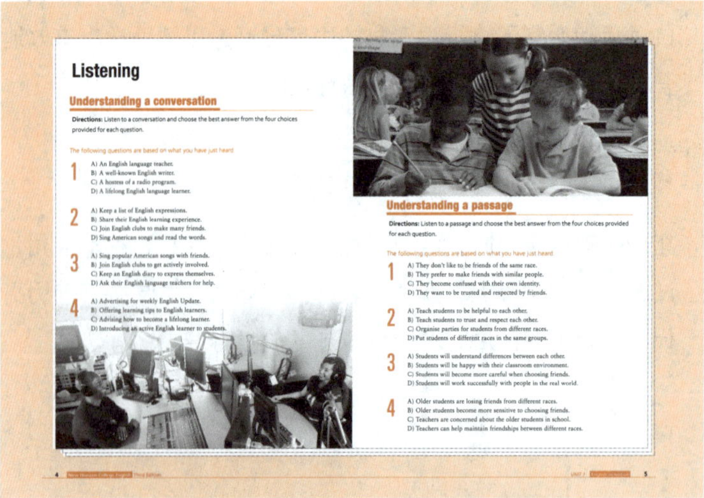

Listening

Understanding a conversation

Directions: Listen to a conversation and choose the best answer from the four choices provided for each question.

The following questions are based on what you have just heard.

1
A) An English language teacher.
B) A well-known English writer.
C) A hostess of a radio program.
D) A lifelong English language learner.

2
A) Keep a list of English expressions.
B) Share their English learning experience.
C) Join English clubs to make many friends.
D) Sing American songs and read the words.

3
A) Sing popular American songs with friends.
B) Join English clubs to get actively involved.
C) Keep an English diary to express themselves.
D) Ask their English language teachers for help.

4
A) Advertising for weekly English Update.
B) Offering learning tips to English learners.
C) Advising how to become a lifelong learner.
D) Introducing an active English learner to students.

4

Understanding a passage

Directions: Listen to a passage and choose the best answer from the four choices provided for each question.

The following questions are based on what you have just heard.

1
A) They don't like to be friends of the same race.
B) They prefer to make friends with similar people.
C) They become confused with their own identity.
D) They want to be trusted and respected by friends.

2
A) Teach students to be helpful to each other.
B) Teach students to trust and respect each other.
C) Organise parties for students from different races.
D) Put students of different races in the same groups.

3
A) Students will understand differences between each other.
B) Students will be happy with their classroom environment.
C) Students will become more careful when choosing friends.
D) Students will work successfully with people in the real world.

4
A) Older students are losing friends from different races.
B) Older students become more sensitive to choosing friends.
C) Teachers are concerned about the older students in school.
D) Teachers can help maintain friendships between different races.

5

Speaking

- **Practicing conversational skills**

设计语言功能训练板块，提供常用交际表达用语、示范性对话和实战对话演练，帮助学生灵活运用所学语言表达与会话策略。

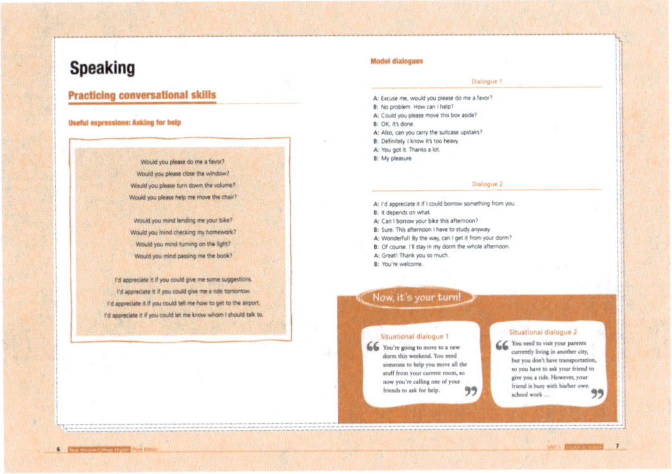

Speaking

Practicing conversational skills

Useful expressions: Asking for help

Would you please do me a favor?
Would you please close the window?
Would you please turn down the volume?
Would you please help me move the chair?

Would you mind lending me your bike?
Would you mind checking my homework?
Would you mind turning on the light?
Would you mind passing me the book?

I'd appreciate it if you could give me some suggestions.
I'd appreciate it if you could give me a ride tomorrow.
I'd appreciate it if you could tell me how to get to the airport.
I'd appreciate it if you could let me know whom I should talk to.

Model dialogues

Dialogue 1

A: Excuse me, would you please do me a favor?
B: No problem. How can I help?
A: Could you please move this box aside?
B: OK, it's done.
A: Also, can you carry the suitcase upstairs?
B: Definitely. I know it's too heavy.
A: You got it. Thanks a lot.
B: My pleasure.

Dialogue 2

A: I'd appreciate it if I could borrow something from you.
B: It depends on what.
A: Can I borrow your bike this afternoon?
B: Sure. This afternoon I have to study anyway.
A: Wonderful! By the way, can I get it from your dorm?
B: Of course. I'll stay in my dorm the whole afternoon.
A: Great! Thank you so much.
B: You're welcome.

Now, it's your turn!

Situational dialogue 1

"You're going to move to a new dorm this weekend. You need someone to help you move all the stuff from your current room, so now you're calling one of your friends to ask for help."

Situational dialogue 2

"You need to visit your parents currently living in another city, but you don't have transportation, so you have to ask your friend to give you a ride. However, your friend is busy with his/her own school work ..."

6 7

- **Listening and speaking**

每单元包含长对话、篇章各一篇，听听说说，听说结合。听力练习形式多样，帮助学生提升听力技巧、内化语言知识；口语活动紧密联系听力短文，包含讨论开放式问题、复述故事等，输入与输出有机融合，以有效提高语言应用能力。

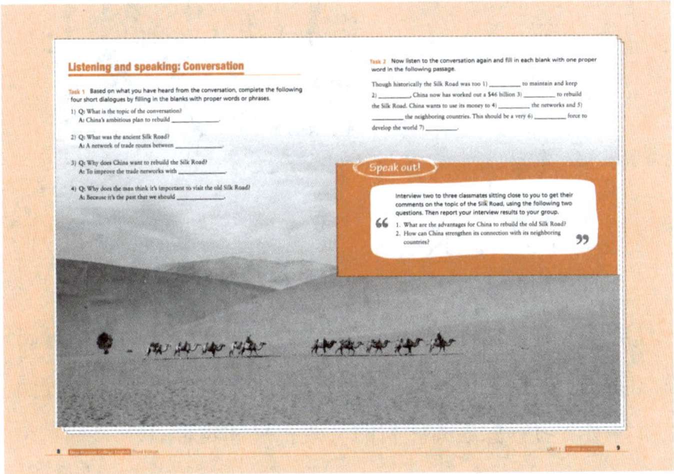

Listening and speaking: Conversation

Task 1 Based on what you have heard from the conversation, complete the following four short dialogues by filling in the blanks with proper words or phrases.

1) Q: What is the topic of the conversation?
A: China's ambitious plan to rebuild ________.

2) Q: What was the ancient Silk Road?
A: A network of trade routes between ________.

3) Q: Why does China want to rebuild the Silk Road?
A: To improve the trade networks with ________.

4) Q: Why does the man think it's important to visit the old Silk Road?
A: Because it's the past that we should ________.

Task 2 Now listen to the conversation again and fill in each blank with one proper word in the following passage.

Though historically the Silk Road was too 1) ________ to maintain and keep 2) ________, China now has worked out a $46 billion 3) ________ to rebuild the Silk Road. China wants to use its money to 4) ________ the networks and 5) ________ the neighboring countries. This should be a very 6) ________ force to develop the world 7) ________.

Speak out!

Interview two to three classmates sitting close to you to get their comments on the topic of the Silk Road, using the following two questions. Then report your interview results to your group.

1. What are the advantages for China to rebuild the old Silk Road?
2. How can China strengthen its connection with its neighboring countries?

8 9

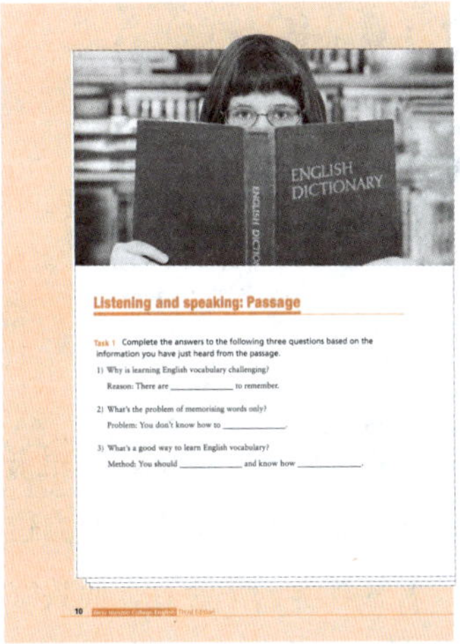

Listening and speaking: Passage

Task 1 Complete the answers to the following three questions based on the information you have just heard from the passage.

1) Why is learning English vocabulary challenging?
Reason: There are ________ to remember.

2) What's the problem of memorising words only?
Problem: You don't know how to ________.

3) What's a good way to learn English vocabulary?
Method: You should ________ and know how ________.

10

Unit report

基于单元主题，每单元设置口头汇报任务，引导学生表达个人观点，在提高口语表达能力的同时，培养思辨能力、沟通能力和组织能力等，全面提升学生的综合素养。

UNIT REPORT

You're required to prepare a two-minute speech on one of the following topics regarding learning English or any topic related to the unit theme. You will be asked to present it in the next class.

- My language barrier
- My language experience
- My learning strategies

Sample:

Hello, everyone. I have so much to say about my English learning experience, but to cut it short, let me start with the importance of everyday practice. Everyone knows that the more English we hear, the easier it will be for us to understand. So, when I was traveling in the US last summer, I tried to start with easy things. I asked questions at stores or asked where I could find something. I also said "hello" to bus drivers. I tried to open my mouth whenever I could. I was advised not to worry about making mistakes. It's very true. To me, it's not important how many mistakes I make. The most important is how much I can speak. Thank you!

12

Homework

每单元提供的素材类型包括新闻报道和篇章，支持学生进行课外训练，以有效提升自主学习能力。

Homework

Section A: Understanding news reports

News report 1

Directions: Now you will hear a news report. At the end of the report, you will hear some questions. After you hear a question, choose the best answer from the four choices.

The following questions are based on what you have just heard.

1
A) To invite as many people as possible.
B) To remind people not to waste money.
C) To rent a wedding dress to save money.
D) To spend a lot of money on their wedding.

2
A) They bought the bride a used wedding dress.
B) They entertained the guests with unused food.
C) They asked a local charity to collect unused food.
D) They sent digital wedding invitations to the guests.

3
A) Many guests applauded the couple's decision.
B) Many guests were unhappy about the wedding.
C) The couple saved money and the earth as well.
D) The couple received criticism from their guests.

13

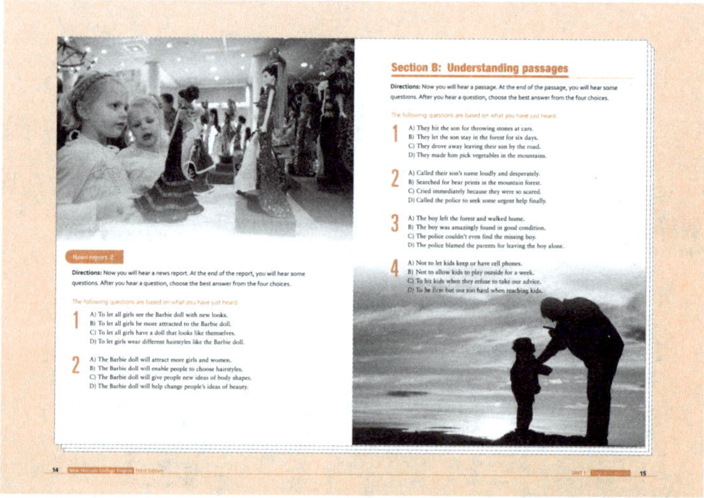

News report 2

Directions: Now you will hear a news report. At the end of the report, you will hear some questions. After you hear a question, choose the best answer from the four choices.

The following questions are based on what you have just heard.

1
A) To let all girls see the Barbie doll with new looks.
B) To let all girls be more attracted to the Barbie doll.
C) To let all girls have a doll that looks like themselves.
D) To let girls wear different hairstyles like the Barbie doll.

2
A) The Barbie doll will attract more girls and women.
B) The Barbie doll will enable people to choose hairstyles.
C) The Barbie doll will give people new ideas of body shapes.
D) The Barbie doll will help change people's ideas of beauty.

Section B: Understanding passages

Directions: Now you will hear a passage. At the end of the passage, you will hear some questions. After you hear a question, choose the best answer from the four choices.

The following questions are based on what you have just heard.

1
A) They hit the son for throwing stones at cars.
B) They let the son stay in the forest for six days.
C) They drove away leaving their son by the road.
D) They made him pick vegetables in the mountains.

2
A) Called their son's name loudly and desperately.
B) Searched for bear prints in the mountain forest.
C) Cried immediately because they were so scared.
D) Called the police to seek some urgent help finally.

3
A) The boy left the forest and walked home.
B) The boy was amazingly found in good condition.
C) The police couldn't even find the missing boy.
D) The police blamed the parents for leaving the boy alone.

4
A) Not to let kids keep or have cell phones.
B) Not to allow kids to play outside for a week.
C) To hit kids when they refuse to take our advice.
D) To be firm but not too hard when teaching kids.

14

15

3 教材资源

《听说教程》提供教师用书、学习光盘、教学课件等配套资源，内容与学生用书互为巩固和补充，对教学进行全方位支持；同时，提供立体、便捷的外语数字化教学平台（U 校园智慧教学云平台），使数字课程和移动学习资源成为教材的有效扩展和延伸。

通过 U 校园平台，《听说教程》的数字课程能提供更丰富的学习资源和学习工具，使学生在课堂学习之外，还能进行多样化、个性化的自我训练和提高。对于角色扮演等口语活动提供语音评测，通过多维度的反馈帮助学生提升语音语调。同时，平台还为教师提供了丰富的试题库资源，包含多种体裁类型的听力测试题，教师可根据需要，自行选择、组卷，及时评估和考查学习情况。此外，《听说教程》（第三版）开创性地设计和研发了基于移动终端的学习资源，包括移动端数字课程和外研随身学 App 等，帮助学生充分利用碎片化时间学习，培养自主学习习惯，提高自主学习能力。

各高校可根据本校实际教学需要选择不同的资源组合方式，使教材与数字课程相结合，课堂教学与自主学习相结合，为教师和学生提供立体化、个性化的开放教学空间。

《新视野大学英语（第三版）听说教程》系列教材的总主编为上海交通大学郑树棠教授。各级别负责人分别为丁雅萍、盈文、吴勇和金霞。

《新视野大学英语（第三版）听说教程 2》主编为郑树棠、盈文。编写人员有郑树棠、盈文、董美英、汪东萍、马琴、郭遂红、苏鹏等。

《新视野大学英语（第三版）听说教程 2》由郑树棠审定全稿。

本书在编写中得到了外籍专家 Rita Kahn 的大力支持和帮助，在此表示衷心的感谢。

《新视野大学英语（第三版）听说教程 2》在编写过程中还得到刘雅敏、饶小飞等人的帮助，在此一并致谢。

编 者

2017 年 5 月

CONTENTS

UNIT 1

English in motion

Warm-up

Directions: You will listen to a conversation between two friends about learning English. After listening, complete the exercises in "What did you hear?" and "How would you respond?"

1 What did you hear?

Choose the correct answer based on what you heard from the conversation.

1) How can we make learning English more interesting?
   A) Take weekly English class.
   B) Determine our learning style.
   C) Have conversations with people.

2) How can we make learning English more effective?
   A) Talk to the people in bookstores.
   B) Make adventures anywhere we go.
   C) Surround ourselves with English.

2 How would you respond?

Please give your personal opinions by choosing one of the letters in each group.

1) What do you think about learning English?
   A) Easy.
   B) Difficult.
   C) So-so.

2) How can you make learning English an adventure?
   A) Seek every chance to speak English.
   B) Look for English everywhere around us.
   C) Practice what we have learned in class.

Listening

Understanding a conversation

Directions: Listen to a conversation and choose the best answer from the four choices provided for each question.

The following questions are based on what you have just heard.

1
A) An English language teacher.
B) A well-known English writer.
C) A hostess of a radio program.
D) A lifelong English language learner.

2
A) Keep a list of English expressions.
B) Share their English learning experience.
C) Join English clubs to make many friends.
D) Sing American songs and read the words.

3
A) Sing popular American songs with friends.
B) Join English clubs to get actively involved.
C) Keep an English diary to express themselves.
D) Ask their English language teachers for help.

4
A) Advertising for weekly English Update.
B) Offering learning tips to English learners.
C) Advising how to become a lifelong learner.
D) Introducing an active English learner to students.

Understanding a passage

Directions: Listen to a passage and choose the best answer from the four choices provided for each question.

The following questions are based on what you have just heard.

1
A) They don't like to be friends of the same race.
B) They prefer to make friends with similar people.
C) They become confused with their own identity.
D) They want to be trusted and respected by friends.

2
A) Teach students to be helpful to each other.
B) Teach students to trust and respect each other.
C) Organise parties for students from different races.
D) Put students of different races in the same groups.

3
A) Students will understand differences between each other.
B) Students will be happy with their classroom environment.
C) Students will become more careful when choosing friends.
D) Students will work successfully with people in the real world.

4
A) Older students are losing friends from different races.
B) Older students become more sensitive to choosing friends.
C) Teachers are concerned about the older students in school.
D) Teachers can help maintain friendships between different races.

Speaking

Practicing conversational skills

Useful expressions: Asking for help

Would you please do me a favor?
Would you please close the window?
Would you please turn down the volume?
Would you please help me move the chair?

Would you mind lending me your bike?
Would you mind checking my homework?
Would you mind turning on the light?
Would you mind passing me the book?

I'd appreciate it if you could give me some suggestions.
I'd appreciate it if you could give me a ride tomorrow.
I'd appreciate it if you could tell me how to get to the airport.
I'd appreciate it if you could let me know whom I should talk to.

Model dialogues

Dialogue 1

A: Excuse me, would you please do me a favor?
B: No problem. How can I help?
A: Could you please move this box aside?
B: OK, it's done.
A: Also, can you carry the suitcase upstairs?
B: Definitely. I know it's too heavy.
A: You got it. Thanks a lot.
B: My pleasure.

Dialogue 2

A: I'd appreciate it if I could borrow something from you.
B: It depends on what.
A: Can I borrow your bike this afternoon?
B: Sure. This afternoon I have to study anyway.
A: Wonderful! By the way, can I get it from your dorm?
B: Of course. I'll stay in my dorm the whole afternoon.
A: Great! Thank you so much.
B: You're welcome.

Now, it's your turn!

Situational dialogue 1

"You're going to move to a new dorm this weekend. You need someone to help you move all the stuff from your current room, so now you're calling one of your friends to ask for help."

Situational dialogue 2

"You need to visit your parents currently living in another city, but you don't have transportation, so you have to ask your friend to give you a ride. However, your friend is busy with his/her own school work ..."

Listening and speaking: Conversation

Task 1 Based on what you have heard from the conversation, complete the following four short dialogues by filling in the blanks with proper words or phrases.

1) **Q:** What is the topic of the conversation?
   A: China's ambitious plan to rebuild ________________.

2) **Q:** What was the ancient Silk Road?
   A: A network of trade routes between ________________.

3) **Q:** Why does China want to rebuild the Silk Road?
   A: To improve the trade networks with ________________.

4) **Q:** Why does the man think it's important to visit the old Silk Road?
   A: Because it's the past that we should ________________.

Task 2 Now listen to the conversation again and fill in each blank with one proper word in the following passage.

Though historically the Silk Road was too 1) __________ to maintain and keep 2) __________, China now has worked out a $46 billion 3) __________ to rebuild the Silk Road. China wants to use its money to 4) __________ the networks and 5) __________ the neighboring countries. This should be a very 6) __________ force to develop the world 7) __________.

Speak out!

Interview two to three classmates sitting close to you to get their comments on the topic of the Silk Road, using the following two questions. Then report your interview results to your group.

1. What are the advantages for China to rebuild the old Silk Road?
2. How can China strengthen its connection with its neighboring countries?

Listening and speaking: Passage

Task 1 Complete the answers to the following three questions based on the information you have just heard from the passage.

1) Why is learning English vocabulary challenging?

   Reason: There are ______________ to remember.

2) What's the problem of memorising words only?

   Problem: You don't know how to ______________.

3) What's a good way to learn English vocabulary?

   Method: You should ______________ and know how ______________.

Task 2 Now listen to the passage again. Based on what you have heard from the passage, match the left with the right to combine the following sentences.

1) When only memorising a list of words, ______.

2) When using the words every day, ______.

3) When seeing the words in a story, ______.

a you understand better how they are used.

b you become more confident about using them.

c you may not be able to use "thin" or "narrow" correctly.

Speak out!

"Now the class will be divided into two because you'll be engaged in a mini-debate: Can students learn vocabulary more effectively through actually using them in everyday life? Whether you're in the group of pros or the group of cons, you must present your ideas within the assigned time."

UNIT REPORT

You're required to prepare a two-minute speech on one of the following topics regarding learning English or any topic related to the unit theme. You will be asked to present it in the next class.

- My language barrier
- My language experience
- My learning strategies

Sample:

Hello, everyone. I have so much to say about my English learning experience, but to cut it short, let me start with the importance of everyday practice. Everyone knows that the more English we hear, the easier it will be for us to understand. So, when I was traveling in the US last summer, I tried to start with easy things. I asked questions at stores or asked where I could find something. I also said "hello" to bus drivers. I tried to open my mouth whenever I could. I was advised not to worry about making mistakes. It's very true. To me, it's not important how many mistakes I make. The most important is how much I can speak. Thank you!

Homework

Section A: Understanding news reports

News report 1

Directions: Now you will hear a news report. At the end of the report, you will hear some questions. After you hear a question, choose the best answer from the four choices.

The following questions are based on what you have just heard.

1
A) To invite as many people as possible.
B) To remind people not to waste money.
C) To rent a wedding dress to save money.
D) To spend a lot of money on their wedding.

2
A) They bought the bride a used wedding dress.
B) They entertained the guests with unused food.
C) They asked a local charity to collect unused food.
D) They sent digital wedding invitations to the guests.

3
A) Many guests applauded the couple's decision.
B) Many guests were unhappy about the wedding.
C) The couple saved money and the earth as well.
D) The couple received criticism from their guests.

News report 2

Directions: Now you will hear a news report. At the end of the report, you will hear some questions. After you hear a question, choose the best answer from the four choices.

The following questions are based on what you have just heard.

1
A) To let all girls see the Barbie doll with new looks.
B) To let all girls be more attracted to the Barbie doll.
C) To let all girls have a doll that looks like themselves.
D) To let girls wear different hairstyles like the Barbie doll.

2
A) The Barbie doll will attract more girls and women.
B) The Barbie doll will enable people to choose hairstyles.
C) The Barbie doll will give people new ideas of body shapes.
D) The Barbie doll will help change people's ideas of beauty.

Section B: Understanding passages

Directions: Now you will hear a passage. At the end of the passage, you will hear some questions. After you hear a question, choose the best answer from the four choices.

The following questions are based on what you have just heard.

1
A) They hit the son for throwing stones at cars.
B) They let the son stay in the forest for six days.
C) They drove away leaving their son by the road.
D) They made him pick vegetables in the mountains.

2
A) Called their son's name loudly and desperately.
B) Searched for bear prints in the mountain forest.
C) Cried immediately because they were so scared.
D) Called the police to seek some urgent help finally.

3
A) The boy left the forest and walked home.
B) The boy was amazingly found in good condition.
C) The police couldn't even find the missing boy.
D) The police blamed the parents for leaving the boy alone.

4
A) Not to let kids keep or have cell phones.
B) Not to allow kids to play outside for a week.
C) To hit kids when they refuse to take our advice.
D) To be firm but not too hard when teaching kids.

UNIT 2

A balanced education

Warm-up

Directions: You will hear an interview between a news program hostess and a student leader from a local university. After listening to the interview, complete the exercises in "What did you hear?" and "How would you respond?"

1 What did you hear?

Choose the correct answer based on what you heard from the conversation.

1) Why has the university fired four professors?
   A) Because the university doesn't think they are important.
   B) Because the university doesn't think they are good to students.
   C) Because the university doesn't think their program is important.

2) What do the students think about the program?
   A) The program provides the most important courses.
   B) The program brings together science and creativity.
   C) The program teaches students some interesting ideas.

2 How would you respond?

Please give your personal opinions by choosing one of the letters in each group.

1) Should the university dismiss these professors?
   A) Yes.
   B) No.
   C) Probably.

2) Should students feel upset and hold a big rally?
   A) Yes.
   B) No.
   C) Probably.

3) Would you support the student rally?
   A) Yes.
   B) No.
   C) Probably.

Listening

Understanding a conversation

Directions: Listen to a conversation and choose the best answer from the four choices provided for each question.

The following questions are based on what you have just heard.

1
A) The new courses related to her major.
B) The extra course "Women's Studies".
C) The required courses on her new schedule.
D) All of the extra courses offered on campus.

2
A) He finds many extra courses very interesting.
B) He easily gets bored when taking extra courses.
C) He enjoys taking the course "Women's Studies".
D) He's never thought about women's topics deeply.

3
A) Because she has three sisters to take care of.
B) Because it helps her to talk with other women.
C) Because it helps people work together in peace.
D) Because she already knows everything about women.

4
A) Extra courses can be very enjoyable.
B) Extra courses can be hard to register for.
C) Students are bored in the extra courses.
D) Students should take "Women's Studies".

Understanding a passage

Directions: Listen to a passage and choose the best answer from the four choices provided for each question.

The following questions are based on what you have just heard.

1
A) They should enjoy playing against their equals.
B) They should be happy to lose their extra weight.
C) They should be older and have good friendships.
D) They should be physically strong and very skilled.

2
A) Most of them will go to a weight-loss centre.
B) Most of them will not play football anymore.
C) Most of them will create a special football league.
D) Most of them will embarrass the younger football players.

3
A) He wanted to play with people who are younger.
B) He wanted to make friends with the team members.
C) He couldn't find an interesting way to lose weight.
D) He was sure that his football league would be successful.

4
A) Because the US has a similar league.
B) Because the players have good friendships.
C) Because 95% of the team players like their team.
D) Because 95% of the team players have lost weight.

Speaking

Practicing conversational skills

Useful expressions: Making complaints

Would you mind not making so much noise?
Would you mind not talking so fast?
Would you mind not giving me so much trouble?
Would you mind not keeping me waiting so long?

I noticed that there was a defect on the bag.
I noticed that this dress had a stain after I bought it.
I've noticed that there is a mistake on the phone bill.
I've noticed the air-conditioner has not been working properly.

I can't help complaining about the terrible dish.
I can't help complaining about the mistake you made.
I can't help complaining about the unsatisfactory service.
I can't help complaining about the bad quality of the product.

Model dialogues

Dialogue 1

A: Sir, would you mind not smoking here?
B: Sorry. Isn't it a smoking zone?
A: Actually it's not.
B: Do you happen to know where it is?
A: It's right over there.
B: Do you mean the open area next to the library?
A: You got it.
B: Oh, I didn't know that. Thanks a lot.

Dialogue 2

A: You look unhappy. Is there anything wrong with the meal?
B: I'm afraid my steak is overdone.
A: Do you mean it's too tough?
B: Right. It doesn't taste good.
A: Sorry about that. May I bring you a new one?
B: If it's not too inconvenient to you.
A: Not a bit, believe me. Just wait a moment.
B: Sure. Really appreciate it.

Now, it's your turn!

Situational dialogue 1

"You would like to make a phone call to your friend using your home phone, but there was a connection problem – a loud echo so you couldn't hear well. You're now complaining to one of the customer service representatives of a phone company."

Situational dialogue 2

"You bought a textbook online from Amazon. Your purchase was supposed to arrive two days ago, but you still haven't received it yet. Therefore, you are now complaining to the online customer service representative about the delay."

Listening and speaking: Conversation

Task 1 Based on what you have heard from the conversation, complete the following sentences by filling in the blanks with proper words or phrases.

1) The woman who speaks is ________________.

2) The purpose of the survey is to get opinions of ________________.

3) The construction of the new shopping centre will be finished in ________________.

Task 2 Now listen to the conversation again. After listening, complete the following chart with the information you've heard regarding the man's opinion about the new shopping centre.

Topic	Opinion	Reason
colour	pleasant but ______	doesn't look serious for ______
design	very modern	prefer ______ design
a small park	______	has some ______ to relax
Starbucks	______ but not a ______	______ other family tea and coffee shops

Speak out!

Discuss the following questions in your group. They are all open-ended, so don't worry about whether what you say is correct or not.

1. What does the interview about the construction of the shopping centre remind you of the area where you live?
2. If there is a shopping centre being built nearby your home, would you like it to include a small park or a Starbucks? Why or why not?
3. Will all the new constructions in cities or rural areas benefit people? Why or why not?

Listening and speaking: Passage

Task 1 Based on what you have heard from the passage, fill in the blanks with proper words or phrases to complete the following two sentences.

The courses of humanities are good for students to take for two main reasons:

1) Help students learn more about __________ and the __________ around them.

2) Help students make ______________ that benefit ______________ around the world.

Task 2 Now listen to the passage again and answer the following questions by filling in the blanks with proper words or phrases.

1) Q: What did studies show about studying humanities?
   A: It helps students to improve their ________________.

2) Q: What advice do researchers give students?
   A: It's better to study a subject that they ___________.

3) Q: What's the purpose of gaining knowledge in sciences?
   A: To help students see how it improves ________________.

Speak out!

"Parents and teachers alike have encouraged young adults to take up subjects that will bring them successful careers. Many parents want their children to be doctors or engineers, not artists or writers. Is what you want to do for your future against your parents' will or expectation? In your group, share your story with each other."

UNIT REPORT

You're required to prepare a two-minute speech on one of the following topics or any topic related to the unit theme. You will be asked to present it in the next class.

- What I dream for my future career
- Why I major in liberal arts
- Whether or not college is worth the money

Sample:

Hello, everyone. What I would like to share today is my personal experiences in taking college courses. When entering college, I chose math as my major because I always wanted to be a math teacher. However, in my first year when I was taking an art history class, I found that my interest was more in arts than in math. I still remember how fascinated I felt when I was listening to the lectures. I felt like I was visiting different places and cultures. I realized that while science courses could let us learn facts and theories, art courses could connect us to the past, the present, and the future. Now, I believe liberal arts courses can bring us more value and more creativity. Thank you.

Homework

Section A: Understanding news reports

News report 1

Directions: Now you will hear a news report. At the end of the report, you will hear some questions. After you hear a question, choose the best answer from the four choices.

The following questions are based on what you have just heard.

1
A) Not to take their children to work.
B) Not to easily show their emotions.
C) Not to discuss their children too much.
D) Not to ask for promotions in their career.

2
A) They are caring fathers.
B) They are weak in character.
C) They are strong in character.
D) They are more open-minded.

News report 2

Directions: Now you will hear a news report. At the end of the report, you will hear some questions. After you hear a question, choose the best answer from the four choices.

The following questions are based on what you have just heard.

1
A) Everyone enjoys doing different daily exercises.
B) Everyone enjoys taking hot baths on a daily basis.
C) Sitting in hot baths has similar benefits as exercising.
D) Sitting in hot baths for one hour makes one relaxed.

2
A) Hot baths decrease the use of body's energy.
B) Hot baths increase the use of body's energy.
C) Hot baths help protect the body from the cold.
D) Hot baths help release more sugar in the blood.

Section B: Understanding passages

Directions: Now you will hear a passage. At the end of the passage, you will hear some questions. After you hear a question, choose the best answer from the four choices.

The following questions are based on what you have just heard.

1
A) To play with his grandparents' dog in the yard.
B) To tell his grandparents about sports and school.
C) To teach his grandparents how to use technology.
D) To have a close relationship with his grandparents.

2
A) Boring since they never asked him about school or sports.
B) Generous because they allowed him to play outside.
C) Not smart because they didn't know any technology.
D) Smart though they often asked him the same questions.

3
A) Because his grandparents didn't teach him anything.
B) Because his grandparents had a secret he didn't know.
C) Because his grandfather was good at writing a report.
D) Because his grandfather's life had been very interesting.

UNIT 3

A fork in the road

Warm-up

Directions: You will listen to a short speech by the Dean of Humanities at a local university. After listening, complete the exercises in "What did you hear?" and "How would you respond?"

1 What did you hear?

Fill in the blanks with the information you heard.

1) Q: When will the students start their next important life stage?
   A: When they finish their __________ and get their __________.

2) Q: What if the students have no idea what to do in the future?
   A: They don't need to worry because they still have time to figure out ______________.

2 How would you respond?

Please choose all that apply to you in each group.

1) What do you think you will achieve in college?
   - ☐ Receive a college degree.
   - ☐ Gain a lot of useful knowledge.
   - ☐ Learn communication skills.
   - ☐ Make friends from different places.
   - ☐ Become more independent.

2) What do you plan to do in the next important part of your life?
   - ☐ Go to graduate school.
   - ☐ Search for a job I like.
   - ☐ Start my own business.
   - ☐ Travel and see the world.
   - ☐ Settle down and have a family.

Listening

Understanding a conversation

Directions: Listen to a conversation and choose the best answer from the four choices provided for each question.

The following questions are based on what you have just heard.

1
A) He was thinking about his studies.
B) He was thinking about his future.
C) He was thinking about his brother.
D) He was thinking if he could get a job.

2
A) He is unhappy and hates his job.
B) He doesn't have a college degree.
C) He has to spend much time working.
D) He never wants to do something fun.

3
A) To work hard to get an ideal job.
B) To get a job right after graduation.
C) To be more realistic to face his life.
D) To take a break before starting a job.

4
A) To take a one-year break after graduation.
B) To learn things he can't learn from a book.
C) To have a balanced life with work and rest.
D) To travel to the places he has never been to.

Understanding a passage

Directions: Listen to a passage and choose the best answer from the four choices provided for each question.

The following questions are based on what you have just heard.

1
A) To follow examples.
B) To follow directions.
C) To follow other people.
D) To follow one's instinct.

2
A) People would easily scream if in pain.
B) People would like to see others suffer.
C) People would tend to follow commands.
D) People would care about the pain of others.

3
A) A question of when children grow into adults.
B) A survey of why children listen to their teachers.
C) An experiment on how people react to commands.
D) A discussion on human nature to follow directions.

Speaking

Practicing conversational skills

Useful expressions: Apologizing and regretting

I'm so sorry that I didn't tell you about it sooner.
I'm awfully sorry that I didn't call you earlier.
I'm terribly sorry to keep you waiting.
I'm extremely sorry to wake you up.

I apologize for taking up so much of your time.
I apologize for giving you so much trouble.
I apologize for making such a loud noise.
I apologize for pushing you too much.

I regret I didn't know about it earlier.
I regret I didn't think about it this way.
I regret I have lost such a good chance.
I regret I didn't go with you to the party.

Model dialogues

Dialogue 1

A: Good morning, Peter.
B: Morning, John. Why didn't you come to my birthday party?
A: I'm so sorry, but I had a family emergency.
B: Oh? What happened?
A: I took my grandpa to the emergency room last night.
B: Really? What was wrong with him?
A: He had the stomach flu, but he's in good shape now.
B: What a big relief!

Dialogue 2

A: Hey, Sue. How are you?
B: Very well. And yourself?
A: Just fine. I apologize for not being able to meet up with you guys.
B: Oh, you mean last Saturday?
A: Yes, I was supposed to work with you guys on the group project last Saturday.
B: Don't worry about it. We just put the ideas together and will meet again next Saturday.
A: That's wonderful since I still have chance to do my share.
B: You can say that! Feel better now?
A: Absolutely.

Dialogue 3

A: Hi, Tim. Long time no see!
B: True, it's been ages. How's everything going?
A: I've been super busy these days.
B: Are you kidding? It's still the middle of school break!
A: I've been busy with interviews with a big company.
B: Do you mean the company is now hiring?
A: It was hiring, but it already closed yesterday.
B: That's awful! I regret I didn't know about it earlier.
A: Don't worry. The company will have more job openings soon.
B: Hope so. Would you please let me know when the hiring starts?
A: Sure, I will.

Now, it's your turn!

Situational dialogue 1

"You and your classmate are talking about the traffic this morning. You start with an apology for being late to the group meeting, and your classmate shows understanding of what you said."

Situational dialogue 2

"You are chatting with one of your classmates. Because of the heavy traffic, you couldn't arrive on time to get an interview with a software company. As a result, your name was removed from the interviewee list. You regret that you have missed such a good chance to work in the company."

Listening and speaking: Conversation

Task 1 Based on what you have heard from the interview, complete the following chart with the correct information about Maggie's goals if elected as the president of the student union.

The goals to be accomplished by Maggie:

Plan	Issue	Solution
1	the high cost of attending this university	• work hard to reduce ____________ • find ________________ for students • add more ___________ opportunities
2	current crowded classrooms	• change some courses ________________ • offer some courses ________________

Task 2 Now listen to the conversation again and fill out each blank with proper words or phrases to answer the question: Why did Maggie think she would be the best student union president?

Because she truly ________________ the students at the university and she would ________________ in her power to improve ________________ at this great university.

Speak out!

Suppose you are running for the next year's student union president and you are now presenting in class your short speech (six to eight sentences). You may start your speech with one of the following sentences:

- I would like to run for the student union president because I think I would be a good and responsible president. First,...
- I believe a student union president should know what students really want and how he can meet their needs, so I would first ...

Listening and speaking: Passage

Task 1 Answer the following questions by completing the information you have just heard from the passage.

1) According to the passage, what is an odyssey year?

An odyssey year is a break between ________________, or it's a break between ________________.

2) In what way can odyssey years benefit young adults?

It'll give them a chance to ________________ and become ________________.

Task 2 Now listen to the passage again. Based on what you have heard from the passage, match the left column with the right to present people's different perspectives of odyssey years.

People	Thinking
1) Young adults	a think kids need a controlled environment
2) Many parents	b believe it is not good for everyone
3) Some parents	c feel nervous and not prepared
4) Experts	d worry their kids won't go back to study or work

Speak out!

> Some of you may support the idea to take a one-year break before going to college, just like Malia did, but others may disagree with the idea. Now the whole class starts to debate on the topic: Should Malia take a one-year break to explore her life?

UNIT REPORT

You're required to prepare a two-minute speech on one of the following topics or any topic related to the unit theme. You will be asked to present it in the next class.

- My new life stage
- My study-abroad plan
- My life exploration

Sample:

Hello, everyone. To be honest with you, I'm really confused about the next stage of my life. I don't know the next step down my road: to continue with my study or look for a job to start my career. Both have positive and negative effects. If I go to graduate school, it means I have to be buried in books for another two to three years but will earn a higher degree in the end; if I start to work, I will have more financial freedom but may end up with dead-end jobs. I feel I'm lost. Just like standing at a fork in the road, I simply don't know which way to take. Is it a common phenomenon during the "odyssey years"? You may have the answer. Thanks.

Homework

Section A: Understanding news reports

News report 1

Directions: Now you will hear a news report. At the end of the report, you will hear some questions. After you hear a question, choose the best answer from the four choices.

The following questions are based on what you have just heard.

D.

1
A) Thinking about different ways to save energy.
B) Adding plates to the roof of the airport building.
C) Paying a lot of money for electricity every month.
D) Trying to use energy from the sun's light and heat.

2
A) To hire a company to manage the huge airport.
B) To cut down their investment in an energy system.
C) To put fewer plates on the top of the airport building.
D) To use a huge area nearby to absorb the sun's energy.

News report 2

Directions: Now you will hear a news report. At the end of the report, you will hear some questions. After you hear a question, choose the best answer from the four choices.

The following questions are based on what you have just heard.

1
A) Many department stores in the US are in trouble.
B) Many department stores have better services now.
C) Many department stores have attracted old people.
D) Many department stores no longer display luxuries.

2
A) Customers don't have time to go shopping.
B) Online shopping only attracts young people.
C) Customers spend more time shopping online.
D) Customers don't have money to buy luxuries.

3
A) Help customers to save more money.
B) Find more interesting styles of clothes.
C) Provide a better environment and service.
D) Let customers receive their items at home.

Section B: Understanding passages

Directions: Now you will hear a passage. At the end of the passage, you will hear some questions. After you hear a question, choose the best answer from the four choices.

The following questions are based on what you have just heard.

1
A) Make sounds to meet humans.
B) Use smoke to get rid of the bees.
C) Reward humans with pieces of nest.
D) Take humans to find honey in the nest.

2
A) They often bite bees and then die.
B) They like to eat honey very much.
C) They usually don't like to eat the bees' nest.
D) They cooperate with humans to get food from bees.

3
A) They don't really like to work with humans.
B) They are not very successful finding bees' nest.
C) They understand the special sounds from humans.
D) They respond to different sounds in the same way.

4
A) How humans protect wild birds in Africa.
B) How humans get honey helped by wild birds.
C) How humans help wild birds to get the nest.
D) How humans train wild birds to be responsive.

UNIT 4

Love can wait

Warm-up

Directions: You will listen to a passage about a special high school party. After listening, complete the exercises in "What did you hear?" and "How would you respond?"

1 What did you hear?

Choose the correct answer based on what you heard from the passage.

1) What does the passage say about prom?
   A) It's a party for high school students to make friends.
   B) It's a party for high school students to drink alcohol.
   C) It's a party for high school students to date someone.
   D) It's a party for high school students to have fun as friends.

2) What's more common for boys and girls to do now?
   A) Boys and girls would go to prom with their family.
   B) Boys and girls would go to prom as a group of friends.
   C) A girl would ask her boyfriend to go to prom with her.
   D) A boy would ask his girlfriend to go to prom with him.

2 How would you respond?

Please give your personal opinions by choosing one of the letters in each group.

1) Are there such parties on your campus?
   A) Yes.
   B) No.
   C) Sometimes.

2) Whom do you prefer to go with to such parties?
   A) Go with boyfriends or girlfriends.
   B) Go with a group of friends.
   C) Invite our parents to join us.

Listening

Understanding a conversation

Directions: Listen to a conversation and choose the best answer from the four choices provided for each question.

The following questions are based on what you have just heard.

1
A) Because they are all excited about the baby.
B) Because they are all adults in the family now.
C) Because everyone wants to take care of the baby.
D) Because the baby will bring them a lot of laughter.

2
A) They hope their son can enjoy university now.
B) They think their son should have his career later.
C) They want their son to take time to find someone.
D) They want their son to have his family very soon.

3
A) She was happy to see her son get married.
B) She was excited about her daughter's wedding.
C) She worried that her son would be a bachelor.
D) She worried that her daughter would be single.

4
A) The woman's sister is going to have a baby.
B) It's hard to be a parent and take care of a baby.
C) People take more time to start having a family.
D) People have different opinions about when to get married.

Understanding a passage

Directions: Listen to a passage and choose the best answer from the four choices provided for each question.

The following questions are based on what you have just heard.

1
A) Players may drive around and catch the Pokémon.
B) Players should have a new phone to play the game.
C) Players must walk and move around to play the game.
D) Players have to hide their phone to catch the Pokémon.

2
A) Because the game brings people a lot of fun.
B) Because many children are playing the game.
C) Because it is an enjoyable and exciting game.
D) Because people come together to play the game.

3
A) Players found some animals dead in their cages.
B) Players found some dead bodies and trapped animals.
C) One player was found under some bushes in San Diego.
D) A 19-year-old girl was looking for Pokémon near a river.

4
A) The game has led players to happy discoveries.
B) Many players have fallen down and were injured.
C) The game forces players to get out of their house to play.
D) All players have been careless when they walked around.

Speaking

Practicing conversational skills

Useful expressions: Giving compliments

I like your coat. It looks so beautiful!

I like the style of your dress. It looks good on you!

I like your sweater. It just goes well with your pants.

I like your haircut. It makes you look much younger.

It's fantastic that you got a promotion!

It's wonderful that you'll go on a vacation!

It's excellent that you'll finish your project by next week!

It's amazing that you completed the work ahead of time!

Your leadership ability is incredible!

Your help to the homeless people is valuable.

The house you recently bought is impressive!

The speech you made is really inspirational!

Model dialogues

Dialogue 1

A: I bought a scarf yesterday. Look!
B: Wow, I like it. It feels so warm.
A: Yeah, it's made of wool.
B: Is it? I like the striped pattern also.
A: Thanks. I prefer simple fashion.
B: Me too. Why don't you try it on?
A: Of course. How does it look on me?
B: It looks great on you. Is it a name brand?
A: Yes, but I bought it when it was on sale.
B: Awesome!

Dialogue 2

A: Yolanda, your new apartment looks very nice.
B: Thanks. My parents and I have just moved in.
A: Really? Did you buy it or rent it?
B: We actually bought it this summer.
A: Wonderful! Is it a two-bedroom apartment?
B: Yes, with one living room and one bath.
A: Wow, your living room is spacious.
B: I know. I feel happy about it.
A: Cool. Congratulations!

Now, it's your turn!

Situational dialogue 1

"Today is the first day of school, and all the freshmen are meeting in the classroom. The girl sitting next to you dressed up nicely, so you start giving compliments on the style and color of her dress."

Situational dialogue 2

"In today's class, everyone needs to make a speech, but you're nervous about speaking in front of class. Someone already finished and did a wonderful job, so you're now complimenting his/her report."

Listening and speaking: Conversation

Task 1 Based on what you have heard from the conversation, decide whether the following statements are true (T) or false (F).

1) (T/F) There was a huge fire in California near the woman's home.

2) (T/F) It was very hard for the woman to decide what to take with her.

3) (T/F) The woman couldn't take the things that have special memories.

4) (T/F) The woman cried because her house was really damaged from the fire.

Task 2 Now listen to the conversation again and fill in the blanks with proper words or phrases in the following two short narratives.

1) Facing the dangerous fire and receiving a police warning to leave home, Vivian quickly __________ what is most important to her. The things she tried to pick up are: important documents, computer, photo books, and the things left by ______________.

2) Vivian's neighbor had his house severely __________. However, he said that the house could be __________, but his family could never be replaced. They are safe now, and that's all that __________ to him.

Speak out!

Now you'll comment on the disaster described in the conversation. You may freely respond to the following two questions in class.

1. What do you think of Vivian's reaction to such a huge disaster?
2. What are the most negative consequences of such a disaster?

Listening and speaking: Passage

Task 1 Based on the information you have just heard from the passage, rearrange the time order of the love story by placing a proper number next to each sentence.

☐ Kyle tried to talk to Emma during class.

☐ Emma learned Kyle was a great guy.

☐ Kyle often sat down right next to Emma.

☐ Emma was embarrassed and started to leave.

☐ Kyle and Emma began to date.

☐ Emma was put in a discussion group with Kyle.

[1] It's Emma's first day in college.

Task 2 Now listen to the passage again. Match how Emma reacted to what Kyle did to her before they began to date.

Kyle

Emma

Kyle	Emma
1) "Sorry if I made you feel embarrassed."	a Didn't want to talk to him
2) Sat down right next to Emma	b Didn't pay attention to him
3) Tried to talk to Emma during class	c Thought he was a stupid guy
4) Tried to be Emma's friend	d Stayed since it was too rude to move

Speak out!

"You are now involved in a brainstorming activity in class. You can freely shout out what comes to your mind in order to answer the following two questions.

1. What personal traits should a boy possess to be an ideal male date?
2. What personal traits should a girl possess to be an ideal female date?"

UNIT REPORT

You're required to prepare a two-minute speech on one of the following topics or any topic related to the unit theme. You will be asked to present it in the next class.

- My love story
- Love matters
- An ideal date

Sample:

Hello, everyone. Love is always a hot topic. I often ask myself, "Who is my Mr. Right?" "Should I look for someone who is very rich or very smart?" or "Should I look for someone who loves me but is poor?" The answers to these questions can be varied, depending on what you care about most. To me, my future Mr. Right should be responsible, caring, and humorous. If a person is responsible, he can take care of everything necessary for the family. He should also be caring and considerate. A person won't love you if he only cares about himself. Finally, he should be humorous. A life without jokes is like a banquet without red wine. Therefore, I hope my future Mr. Right has these three personality traits. Thanks.

Homework

Section A: Understanding news reports

News report 1

Directions: Now you will hear a news report. At the end of the report, you will hear some questions. After you hear a question, choose the best answer from the four choices.

The following questions are based on what you have just heard.

1
A) He couldn't get a football shirt from Messi.
B) His family was too poor to buy him a football.
C) He couldn't get a football shirt to look like Messi.
D) His family cannot afford to pay for football lessons.

2
A) The shirt appeared on Facebook.
B) The shirt fit the little boy perfectly.
C) The shirt had blue and white lines on it.
D) The shirt had Messi's name and number on it.

3
A) His picture became very popular on the Internet.
B) Messi met the boy and gave him a football shirt.
C) He knew he could meet Messi someday very soon.
D) He got a real football shirt with Messi's signature.

News report 2

Directions: Now you will hear a news report. At the end of the report, you will hear some questions. After you hear a question, choose the best answer from the four choices.

The following questions are based on what you have just heard.

1
A) By giving them some food.
B) By giving them some money.
C) By giving them haircuts for free.
D) By giving them a chance to talk.

2
A) Because he can practice his skills.
B) Because these people like his haircuts.
C) Because other people don't want to help.
D) Because his help can make them feel good.

Section B: Understanding passages

Directions: Now you will hear a passage. At the end of the passage, you will hear some questions. After you hear a question, choose the best answer from the four choices.

The following questions are based on what you have just heard.

1
A) They made the people near the sea fall sick.
B) They made the fish and birds either sick or die.
C) They gave off bad smells in our natural world.
D) They made people feel like they lived in a trash can.

2
A) Give discounts to those who shop with their own bags.
B) Give extra food to those who shop with their own bags.
C) Tell those who shop without bags to bring them next time.
D) Charge those who shop without bags five pence for each bag.

3
A) Officials are unhappy with the result of this practice.
B) People think that it's of no help to charge extra money.
C) People are now using significantly fewer plastic bags.
D) People still leave 5,000 plastic bags a day on the beaches.

UNIT 5

Money matters

Warm-up

Directions: You will listen to an opening speech on managing money. After listening, complete the exercises in "What did you hear?" and "How would you respond?"

1 What did you hear?

Choose the correct answer based on what you heard from the speech.

1) What's the main purpose of the money from scholarships and loans?
   A) To save the money for personal use.
   B) To pay for school and necessary things.
   C) To freely spend it on anything you wish.

2) Why should college students use credit cards wisely?
   A) To get more financial credit when in college.
   B) To get experience of using credit cards in college.
   C) To avoid huge credit card debts when they graduate.

2 How would you respond?

Please choose what applies to you to answer the following two questions.

1) Do you have much sense of financial freedom now?
   ☐ Yes.
   ☐ No.
   ☐ Hard to say.

2) How would you carefully manage your money?
   ☐ To only buy the things I definitely need.
   ☐ To carefully budget my monthly expenses.
   ☐ To avoid using credit cards if I don't have to.

Listening

Understanding a conversation

Directions: Listen to a conversation and choose the best answer from the four choices provided for each question.

The following questions are based on what you have just heard.

1
A) They're lucky to find a part-time job.
B) They're able to borrow a lot of money.
C) They've paid all their school expenses.
D) They've found campus job information.

2
A) They will borrow more money for another year.
B) They will never start paying back all this money.
C) They will get sick when owing too much money.
D) They will owe a lot of money when they graduate.

3
A) To find a job in the career center.
B) To work a few hours after school.
C) To find a part-time job on campus.
D) To get a job that pays enough money.

4
A) Check online to spend less on what he buys.
B) Stop buying a new cell phone from now on.
C) Stop buying the things he really needs or likes.
D) Stop eating at the café and cook meals himself.

Understanding a passage

Directions: Listen to a passage and choose the best answer from the four choices provided for each question.

The following questions are based on what you have just heard.

1
A) Climbing trees to cut some branches for people.
B) Planting trees near their village in central China.
C) Helping other people to learn how to plant trees.
D) Seeking opportunities to protect the environment.

2
A) The job makes them work very hard.
B) The job helps them live on their own.
C) Both have their physical limitations.
D) Both have to use their feet to do their job.

3
A) They always think about how to get the work done.
B) They always worry if they can complete their work.
C) They depend on friends' help and encouragement.
D) They depend on each other to overcome their limitations.

4
A) They have been offered jobs by many companies.
B) They lost their eyesight due to an accident in 2000.
C) They got injured when they were just three years old.
D) They love the job since it gives them a purpose in life.

Speaking

Practicing conversational skills

Useful expressions: Showing sympathy

I'm truly sorry to hear that.

I'm so sorry to learn about it.

I'm awfully sorry to get this shocking news.

I'm terribly sorry to know that you're having difficulties.

Please convey my sympathy to your friend.

Please extend my sympathy to your family.

Please send my thoughts and prayers to them.

Please remember my thoughts and prayers are with you.

This is a difficult time for you, but please take it easy.

This is a terrible time for you, but please do take care.

This is an uneasy time for you, but everything will be fine.

This is a hard time for you, but you already tried your best.

Model dialogues

Dialogue 1

A: Hello? Who's calling?
B: It's Jenny. How's your mom?
A: Still very ill. Thanks for asking, though.
B: Sorry to hear that. I was hoping she'd be better.
A: Thanks, but she's been receiving good care.
B: Are you the only person taking care of her?
A: My dad also. He hasn't had any sleep yet.
B: Please send him my thoughts and prayers.
A: I surely will. Bye.

Dialogue 2

A: Bryan, I'm awfully sorry about the news.
B: Me, too. Up till now, I still cannot accept the fact.
A: I completely understand your feeling, Bryan.
B: You know, I was brought up by my grandpa.
A: That's very true. I often heard you mention it.
B: So his passing away was a heavy blow on me.
A: It's a difficult time for you, but please take it easy.
B: I will. I know it takes time.
A: Sure. Please don't feel too depressed.
B: Thanks a lot. I'll try my best.

Now, it's your turn!

Situational dialogue 1

"Your classmate's mother was involved in a car accident and got injured. She/he is so worried that she/he cannot concentrate on her/his studies. You feel very sympathetic to her/him. You're now walking out of the classroom with her/him."

Situational dialogue 2

"Your friend has been depressed these days because he/she has just lost a good opportunity to get promoted at his/her work. Being his/her friend, you want to show your sympathy and make him/her feel better, so now you're talking with him/her."

Listening and speaking: Conversation

Task 1 Based on what you have heard from the conversation, answer the following two questions by filling in the blanks with proper words or phrases.

1) What are the two complaints made by the customers?

Complaint 1: The phone operators are __________ to the customers. They are in a hurry to finish the phone call and __________ them whilst they are trying to explain problems.

Complaint 2: The customers are __________ that the ______________ is only two weeks.

2) Why are the operators behaving rudely to customers?

Reason: They're required to help at least ______________ every hour, so they can only spend about ______________ talking to each customer.

Task 2 Now listen to the conversation again and find out how the two issues will be resolved. Then decide whether the following statements are true (T) or false (F).

1) (T/F) The operators will have no more requirements to meet.

2) (T/F) A reasonable number needs to be established.

3) (T/F) The return policy will be changed to 30 days.

4) (T/F) Customers can return products within two months.

5) (T/F) Customers will be happy about the new policy.

Speak out!

"In your group, you'll role-play a meeting with the manager from a local department store. The manager is now getting the customers' feedback on their service. As customers, you want to make complaints. You will complain about what you have personally experienced. The manager needs to take notes while listening to the customers."

Listening and speaking: Passage

Task 1 Based on the information you have just heard from the passage, answer the following two questions by filling in the blanks with proper words or phrases.

1) Q: Why has student spending become a greater concern over the last few years?

   A: Because there is a trend of more ________________ use. More students now have two credit cards. However, they're not ___________ their credit card debt well. Fewer students are looking at their ________________ or paying them on time like they did before.

2) Q: Why are students becoming less responsible than before?

   A: Because some students feel that their debt is ________________, they really don't want to know how much they ___________ and just ignore their debt. There are also many students who have no concept of ___________, so these practices are unfamiliar to them.

Task 2 Now listen to the passage again. After listening, fill in the blanks with the information you have heard.

1) Students are doing ___________ following a budget and saving any money they ___________ from work, school loans and scholarships.

2) Many students don't know how much money is in their ________________ and often don't have enough money in them to ________________.

3) Because students use less cash and ________________ these days, it's harder for students to ________________ how much they're spending.

Speak out!

“Experts believe more schools should offer classes on money management for their students. Do you think it's necessary? Now you'll join the class to debate whether students should be taught how to manage their money.”

UNIT REPORT

You're required to prepare a two-minute speech on one of the following topics or any topic related to the unit theme. You will be asked to present it in the next class.

- My spending habit
- My money management
- A lesson on using money

Sample:

Hello, everyone. Speaking of money management, I want to share with you my opinion. Before I came to college, I had never thought about the money issue. I was always provided with what I needed for school. My parents also gave me monthly allowances. So, I spent the money on my favorite DVDs and electronic products. However, ever since I came to college, I've been having trouble paying my credit card bills. That's because I don't think about how much I've already spent when using my credit card. When the bill comes, I always feel shocked. I could ask my parents for help, but I feel too bad to do it. I know, to be financially independent, I need to learn how to manage my money first. Thank you!

Homework

Section A: Understanding news reports

News report 1

Directions: Now you will hear a news report. At the end of the report, you will hear some questions. After you hear a question, choose the best answer from the four choices.

The following questions are based on what you have just heard.

1
A) Cows are their honoured pets.
B) Cows are their delicious food.
C) Cows are a token of a good life.
D) Cows are not honoured enough by the government.

2
A) They are often washed well to be clean.
B) They cannot be killed and eaten for food.
C) They can't walk around freely by themselves.
D) They walk with a rope around for their safety.

3
A) They worried about the protection of cows.
B) They asked the government to protect cows.
C) People saw them killing the treasured cows.
D) People mistakenly thought they killed cows.

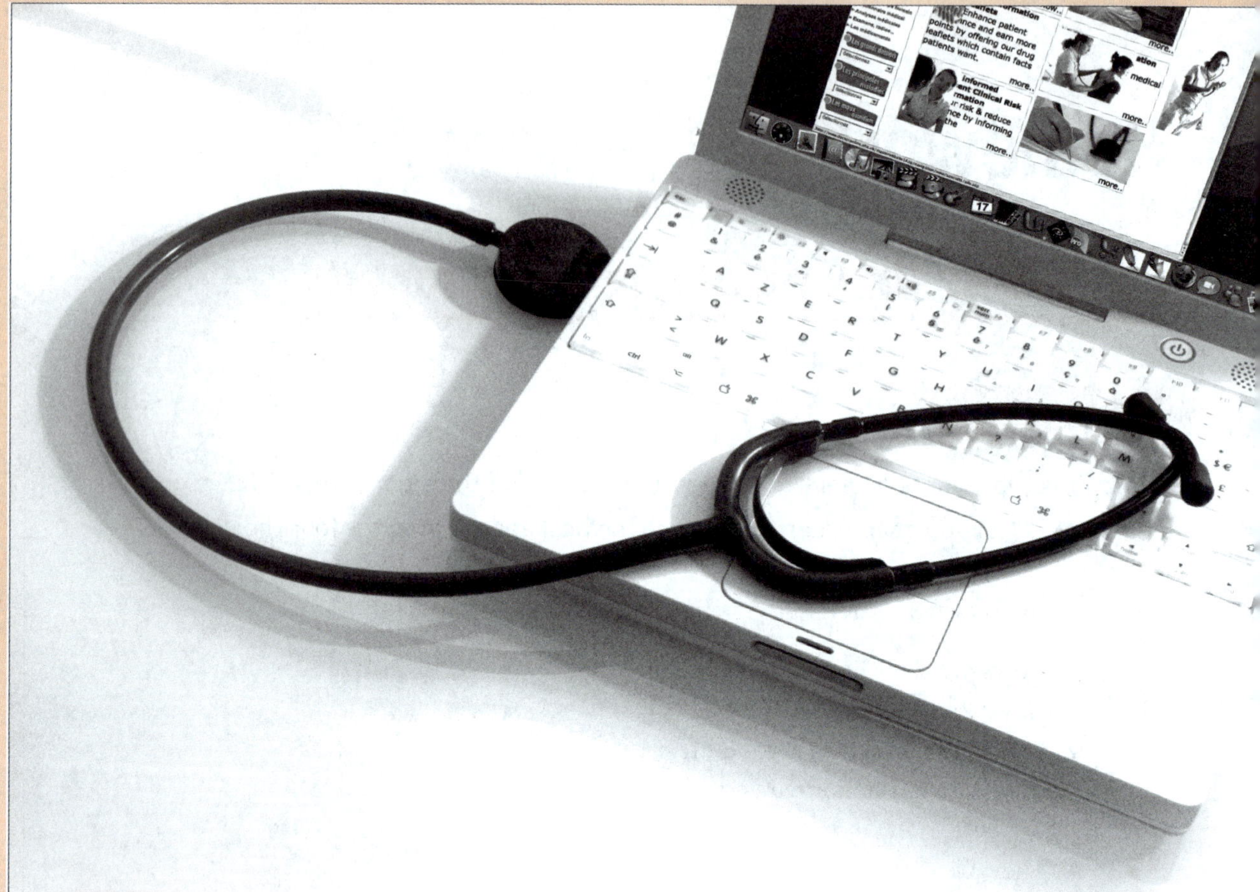

News report 2

Directions: Now you will hear a news report. At the end of the report, you will hear some questions. After you hear a question, choose the best answer from the four choices.

The following questions are based on what you have just heard.

1
A) People use the Internet to seek different advice.
B) People use the Internet to read interesting news.
C) Over half of all adults in the US use the Internet.
D) Over half US adults get medical information online.

2
A) Not many elderly people have Internet service at home.
B) Not many elderly people use online health information.
C) The elderly think online medical advice is very important.
D) The elderly don't really like to use email or online banking.

Section B: Understanding passages

Directions: Now you will hear a passage. At the end of the passage, you will hear some questions. After you hear a question, choose the best answer from the four choices.

The following questions are based on what you have just heard.

1 A) The number of teenagers who have died.
B) The number of teenagers who drink alcohol.
C) The sounds that come from our cell phones.
D) The warnings about not texting while driving.

2 A) Driving a car while drinking alcohol.
B) Writing and sending text messages while driving.
C) Listening to the familiar sound of a text message.
D) Fighting against the desire to check text messages.

3 A) They cannot make a good decision sometimes.
B) They don't have phone software installed in cars.
C) They enjoy the reward chemicals from their brain.
D) They are anxious to text messages to their friends.

4 A) Drivers may look away from the road for just a short moment.
B) Drivers should use a software to prevent themselves using phones.
C) Drivers should put their phones in the trunk before they start driving.
D) Drivers should receive constant warnings about not texting while driving.

UNIT 6

A rich life

Warm-up

Directions: You will listen to a conversation between a man and a woman regarding spending habit. After listening, complete the exercises in "What did you hear?" and "How would you respond?"

1 What did you hear?

Fill in the blanks with the information you have heard.

1) Q: What did the man realise a few months ago?
   A: He realised that he had so many ________________ that he didn't need. He has wasted ________________!

2) Q: What happened to the man in terms of spending money?
   A: He kept buying the latest version of technology every year. Consequently, he drained his ________________ and ended up having no money for ________________. He didn't have any spending money to ________________ either.

2 How would you respond?

Please choose the one that applies to you to answer the following two questions.

1) How often do you feel pressured to buy new products?
   A) All the time.
   B) Sometimes.
   C) Very rare.
   D) Never.

2) Do you feel happy and worried about your finances?
   A) Yes.
   B) No.
   C) Somewhat.

Listening

Understanding a conversation

Directions: Listen to a conversation and choose the best answer from the four choices provided for each question.

The following questions are based on what you have just heard.

1

A) A doctor can live a good life by working hard.
B) A doctor can open many bank accounts freely.
C) A doctor doesn't need to worry about anything.
D) A doctor can always find a job with a good salary.

2

A) He likes to work in an office all day.
B) He likes to work and play outside.
C) He likes young kids' joyful attitudes.
D) He likes young kids' strong opinions.

3

A) Job satisfaction is more important.
B) Work environment is more important.
C) Job security is always more important.
D) A high salary is always more important.

4

A) Seeking advice from his parents first.
B) Having a life that is rich with satisfaction.
C) Searching online to find a well-paying job.
D) Establishing a network through the career center.

Understanding a passage

Directions: Listen to a passage and choose the best answer from the four choices provided for each question.

The following questions are based on what you have just heard.

1
A) Humans with less hair were cleaner.
B) Humans with less hair could run faster.
C) Humans with less hair had lighter skin.
D) Humans with less hair were more attractive.

2
A) Because animals eat more meat than humans.
B) Because animals have more hair than humans.
C) Because animals run much faster than humans.
D) Because animals sweat more effectively than humans.

3
A) They used their hair to keep warm.
B) They lived in small spaces to stay warm.
C) They created fire to cook and keep warm.
D) They consumed meat to keep their body warm.

4
A) Why humans have little hair on their heads.
B) Why humans have little hair on their bodies.
C) Why early humans began to use fire to cook.
D) Why early humans began to hunt for animals.

Speaking

Practicing conversational skills

Useful expressions: Giving advice

If I were you, I would ask someone to give me a ride.
If I were you, I would search online about the company first.
If I were you, I would go shopping when things are on sale.
If I were you, I would consult with my advisor before registration begins.

I think there is no need to take another look.
I think there is no need to ask about his opinion.
I think there is no need to go to graduate school.
I think there is no need to tell him about the incident.

Believe me, it's better to travel with your friends.
Believe me, it's better to do online shopping to save time.
Believe me, it's better to move out when you reach 18.
Believe me, it's better to make a "to do" list before starting a project.

Model dialogues

Dialogue 1

A: Why are you so late, John?
B: I got up late. Sorry about that.
A: Did you oversleep?
B: Not really. I was coughing all night.
A: You mean you couldn't go to sleep?
B: Right. I don't know why I coughed so much. My chest really hurts.
A: If I were you, I would go and see a doctor to get some medicine.
B: I did, but the medicine, for some reason, doesn't help at all.
A: Believe me, you'd better return to the doctor to get a different medicine. The same thing happened to me, and the second medicine helped me a lot.
B: I guess.

Dialogue 2

A: Peter, can you give me some advice about job hunting?
B: Sure, I'd be glad to. What kind of job are you looking for?
A: I love to do consulting but guess I will never get a good consulting job.
B: It's too early to say that. You never know.
A: I've sent out 10 online applications, but no response yet.
B: If I were you, I would touch bases with the companies.
A: Will that give them a negative impression of me?
B: Nope. Believe me, this will leave them a good impression.
A: Really? Then I'll do it to let them know I'm really interested.
B: You got it. One should never say never!

Now, it's your turn!

Situational dialogue 1

"An English exam is coming soon, and your friend feels very worried about the exam because he/she doesn't know how to study for the exam. You advise him/her how to review using the Internet, such as online listening."

Situational dialogue 2

"Your classmate is asking you whether he/she should join the Yoga Club on campus. You're encouraging him/her to do it because it's a good exercise that helps his/her mind and body to relax and release stress."

Listening and speaking: Conversation

Task 1 Based on what you have heard from the conversation, complete the following chart with the correct information about French fries and potato chips.

Food	History
French fries	Though there's some ________ between the French and Belgium over who first made French fries, the popularity of French fries mostly comes from American ____________.
Potato chips	Potato chips seemed to be popular in the US and England ____________, but many people believe an ____________ about how the potato chip was first made.

Task 2 Now listen to the conversation again and rearrange the order of the story according to the time sequence you have heard.

☐ The customer was very particular and said the fries were too soft.
☐ The cook decided to cut the potatoes very, very thin before he fried them.
[1] There was a cook in New York who was making French fries to a customer.
☐ Soon many people eating at the restaurant tried these chips and loved them.
☐ The cook had to make more, but again the customer sent them back to the cook.

Speak out!

"You'll interview three students to get their opinions about the food at McDonald's or any other fast food restaurants in China. Please use the following survey questions.

1. Have you ever been to McDonald's? If yes, how do you like its food?
2. Do you think the food prices at McDonald's are reasonable? Why or why not?"

Listening and speaking: Passage

Task 1 Based on what you have heard from the passage, answer the following two questions by filling in the blanks with proper words or phrases.

1) How do parents mistakenly teach their children to always expect things?
Parents __________ their children for doing something good. For example, parents may buy their children _______________ if they behave nicely or receive _______________ in school.

2) How can the neighborhood in which people live influence their material desires?
If they see their neighbors driving _______________, they feel like they _______________ at the same level as their neighbors or it would be __________.

Task 2 Now listen to the passage again. After listening, decide whether the following statements are true (T) or false (F) based on what you have heard from the passage.

1) (T/F) One of the biggest influences of unnecessary purchases is advertising.

2) (T/F) Advertisements persuade people to purchase more in order to save more.

3) (T/F) If people want to look successful or popular, they should keep buying things.

4) (T/F) Wanting a successful or popular appearance pushes people to work harder.

5) (T/F) Many people don't want to have high credit card debt to just look successful.

Speak out!

"Human desire for material possessions may begin early in life, and this desire will grow into a habit when children grow up. To stop this habit, what can parents do when dealing with their children? Provide your suggestions in the class discussion on this topic."

UNIT REPORT

You're required to prepare a two-minute speech on one of the following topics or any topic related to the unit theme. You will be asked to present it in the next class.

- My opinion about success
- My desire for materialism
- My opinion of advertisements

Sample:

Hello, everyone. I would like to share with you my idea of purchasing designer products. To many men, wearing a name-brand shirt or suit will indirectly show their wealth or success. Similarly, many women are crazy about big name-brand purses. They don't care how much they have to spend. What they care about is the particular purse that will make them look good and eye-catching. However, this kind of thinking doesn't make much sense to me because I think these people treat themselves as a product. They intend to use their appearance to sell themselves. Who cares what you are wearing or carrying in your hands? Maybe some people do, but not me for sure. As long as I'm content with what I have, I feel happy. Thank you.

Homework

Section A: Understanding news reports

News report 1

Directions: Now you will hear a news report. At the end of the report, you will hear some questions. After you hear a question, choose the best answer from the four choices.

The following questions are based on what you have just heard.

1
A) They get the furniture after they are constructed.
B) They get the boxed furniture together with tools.
C) They take the boxed furniture home by themselves.
D) They will receive the boxed furniture in a few weeks.

2
A) It's now making long-lasting furniture.
B) It's now expanding its market to India.
C) It's now producing traditional furniture.
D) It's now producing hand-made furniture.

3
A) They prefer traditional furniture made of wood.
B) They prefer heavy furniture that can last forever.
C) They prefer hand-made furniture that looks nicer.
D) They prefer lighter and more manageable furniture.

News report 2

Directions: Now you will hear a news report. At the end of the report, you will hear some questions. After you hear a question, choose the best answer from the four choices.

The following questions are based on what you have just heard.

1
A) It's a handbag made by an Italian designer.
B) It's the most expensive handbag to be sold.
C) It takes years to make the handmade handbag.
D) It's made of golden leather with diamonds on it.

2
A) People like the things most they cannot get.
B) People can show others that they are very rich.
C) People know these handbags can make a profit.
D) People don't need to be afraid to use it in public.

Section B: Understanding passages

Directions: Now you will hear a passage. At the end of the passage, you will hear some questions. After you hear a question, choose the best answer from the four choices.

The following questions are based on what you have just heard.

1
A) Because they want it to bring more baby rabbits.
B) Because they like the fake rabbit's foot so much.
C) Because they believe it helps them get good luck.
D) Because they think it helps children avoid bad luck.

2
A) Because it's strong enough to keep away bad spirits.
B) Because it looks like the letter "U" on a horse's feet.
C) Because it's strong enough to be above the doorway.
D) Because it protects people when it's hung on the door.

3
A) By avoiding flights on Friday the 13th.
B) By skipping the 13th floor in a building.
C) By being careful on the 13th day of the month.
D) By not talking about the number 13 in religion.

UNIT 7

Gender barriers

Warm-up

Directions: You will listen to a short passage about women's status in society and at work today. After listening, complete the exercises in "What did you hear?" and "How would you respond?"

1 What did you hear?

Decide whether the following statements are true (T) or false (F) according to what you have heard.

1) (T/F) Women can do things other than being a housewife and mother.

2) (T/F) Parents don't want their daughters to be doctors or firefighters.

3) (T/F) Women must make even more changes to be truly equal to men.

4) (T/F) Attitudes towards women at workplace must also be changed.

2 How would you respond?

Please choose the one that applies to you to answer the following two questions.

1) Should women continue working towards equal treatment?
   A) Definitely.
   B) Not really.

2) Should attitudes towards women change in the workplace?
   A) Definitely.
   B) Not really.

Listening

Understanding a conversation

Directions: Listen to a conversation and choose the best answer from the four choices provided for each question.

The following questions are based on what you have just heard.

1
A) She went to Oxford and got a degree in politics.
B) She wasn't interested in becoming a prime minister.
C) She became the first female British prime minister.
D) She had been aiming at becoming a female prime minister.

2
A) Because she spoke out harshly against the Soviet Union.
B) Because she was elected as the first female British prime minister.
C) Because she became a member of British Parliament at 34.
D) Because she didn't care about her duty as a wife and mother.

3
A) She pushed the government a lot to reform.
B) The Russians gave her the name of Iron Lady.
C) She helped the UK win a victory against Argentina.
D) She really helped women to have a voice in politics.

4
A) How Thatcher became popular and won respect.
B) How Thatcher became the British prime minister.
C) Why Thatcher was a woman with strong opinions.
D) Why the woman respected Margaret Thatcher a lot.

Understanding a passage

Directions: Listen to a passage and choose the best answer from the four choices provided for each question.

The following questions are based on what you have just heard.

1
A) Read the online review of the product.
B) Read the online review of the shipping.
C) Write questions about the product online.
D) Write questions about the business online.

2
A) Because bad reviews require legal action.
B) Because bad reviews can hurt their business.
C) Because business reviews are getting popular.
D) Because many people write business reviews.

3
A) Because the business began legal action.
B) Because the business charged them $7,000.
C) Because the couple said the review was true.
D) Because the couple was too sad and unhappy.

4
A) Free speech is protected in the US.
B) The news media can be very helpful.
C) Online reviews can be very powerful.
D) Online reviews can lead to legal action.

Speaking

Practicing conversational skills

Useful expressions: Talking about likes and dislikes

I like fishing, but I don't like hunting.

I like running, but I don't like swimming.

I like playing basketball, but I don't like playing golf.

I like singing, but I don't like dancing or watching TV.

Basketball is his favorite activity. What's yours?

Jogging is his favorite exercise. What's yours?

Playing the piano is her favorite hobby. How about yours?

Watching movies is my favorite activity. How do you like it?

I don't really care much about sports.

I don't really care much about music.

I don't really care much for coffee.

I don't really care much about TV shows.

Model dialogues

Dialogue 1

A: Did you go to the soccer game last Saturday?
B: Yes, my friend gave me a ticket, so I was lucky.
A: How was it? Did you enjoy it?
B: It was wonderful, and I really enjoyed it.
A: I bet you also like to play soccer yourself.
B: Definitely! Soccer is my favorite.
A: Do you also like to play basketball?
B: Unfortunately, I don't really care much for it.
A: That's interesting since many people love the sport.
B: To be honest with you, I'm too short to play it well.

Dialogue 2

A: Do you have any hobbies?
B: Yes, I like playing the piano.
A: Great! Any other hobbies?
B: Sure, listening to music, reading books, and taking pictures.
A: Good. These hobbies can make your life more colorful.
B: Right. I enjoy doing things that can be done by myself alone.
A: I'm just curious. Do you have much time to do what you like?
B: Of course not. I don't have much leisure time. What are your interests?
A: Well, I have a lot of hobbies, but now I'm just crazy about cooking.
B: Wow, cool! I wish I could also learn how to cook my favorite dish.

Now, it's your turn!

Situational dialogue 1

"You and your roommate are talking about whether you should get a dog. Your roommate is fond of pets, so he/she insists that it's a "must do". However, you don't like pets, so you suggest some other things you both like to do."

Situational dialogue 2

"You and your classmate are sharing each other's hobbies. You like to play computer games, shop online, and text your friends. He/she likes to play sports, watch movies and listen to music. You both want to convince each other that your hobbies are more interesting."

Listening and speaking: Conversation

Task 1 Based on what you have heard from the conversation, complete the following sentences by filling in the blanks with proper words or phrases.

1) Some of the issues that may create problems at work include personality __________, lack of __________, and aggressive __________. Also, one interesting problem that can happen at work is __________.

2) It's impossible to make everyone __________ about the temperature in the office. Somebody will always complain that it's ______________, and there's a fight over the ______________.

Task 2 Now listen to the conversation again. After listening, complete the following chart with what was suggested by some studies.

Air conditioner	Suggestion
warmer temperatures	encourage ______________ and ______________ amongst workers
cooler temperatures	help to ______________ and ______________

Speak out!

Work in a small group and discuss the following questions.

“In the conversation, it mentions that women’s bodies don’t produce as much heat as men’s bodies, but the problem is that when people determine the appropriate temperature of the offices, they always use a man’s body heat to decide what the temperature is set at.

Questions:

1. Is it right to set the room temperature according to a man’s body heat? Why or why not?
2. Why do people habitually use a man’s body temperature to set the air conditioner in a room?”

Listening and speaking: Passage

Task 1 Based on what you have heard from the passage, complete the following sentences by filling in the blanks with proper words or phrases.

1) Women around the world are often viewed as ______________ than men, and in some countries, they're considered __________ to give away.

2) India is a country with families that practise traditional ______________ of young girls to older men. The girls must __________ whoever the family has decided to be her husband.

Task 2 Now listen to the passage again and choose the best answer from the three choices provided for each question.

1) Why did the father's family need to find a wife for the father's brother?
   A) He was the oldest child in the family.
   B) He had difficulty finding a pretty wife.
   C) He would make the family lose respect if he is unmarried.

2) Why did the father regret his decision to give his daughter to the man?
   A) The man was uneducated and didn't like to learn.
   B) The man was much older and drank a lot of alcohol.
   C) The man didn't permit the 15-year-old girl to go to school.

Speak out!

Work in a small group and discuss the following question.

"In the passage, it mentions that the father always wanted his daughter to be educated so that she could get rid of the older man and have a bright future. Do you think a woman can always change her fate as long as she is striving to improve her status and becomes well educated?"

UNIT REPORT

You're required to prepare a two-minute speech on one of the following topics or any topic related to the unit theme. You will be asked to present it in the next class.

- My opinion about female bosses
- An ideal future career for a woman
- Should a housewife be respected?

Sample:

Women are born weak in the eyes of many people, but they are definitely not born losers. Even though they're physically not as strong as men, they can be very strong in their mind. They even persevere more than men in certain areas. Take my mom for example. She is a strong woman in my eyes. I remember when I was little, she took over all the household responsibilities despite the fact she needed to commute a long distance to her workplace every early morning, no matter if it was rainy or windy. She tried her best to take care of the family, but she never thought about herself. I was always amazed at her unusual perseverance and motherly care. Therefore, she won my greatest appreciation and respect. Thank you.

Homework

Section A: Understanding news reports

News report 1

Directions: Now you will hear a news report. At the end of the report, you will hear some questions. After you hear a question, choose the best answer from the four choices.

The following questions are based on what you have just heard.

1
A) Causing their children to often miss them.
B) Leaving their children at their friends' home.
C) Not knowing what their children really need.
D) Not spending enough time with their children.

2
A) Technology keeps parents informed of their children.
B) Websites give children information about their parents.
C) Computer programmes help children do different activities.
D) Parents' phones are now updated with children's pictures.

3
A) They should focus on managing the parents.
B) They should focus on caring for the children.
C) They should send more reports to the nursery.
D) They should send more pictures to the parents.

News report 2

Directions: Now you will hear a news report. At the end of the report, you will hear some questions. After you hear a question, choose the best answer from the four choices.

The following questions are based on what you have just heard.

1
A) Because they only judge on skill and intelligence.
B) Because they pay no attention to girls' appearance.
C) Because they present females as objects, not people.
D) Because they stopped using swim wear in contests.

2
A) The contests send the right message to all the young girls.
B) The contests make young girls feel better about themselves.
C) The contests teach these girls how to compete with others.
D) The contests provide enough money for girls to go to college.

Section B: Understanding passages

Directions: Now you will hear a passage. At the end of the passage, you will hear some questions. After you hear a question, choose the best answer from the four choices.

The following questions are based on what you have just heard.

1
A) Play the piano alone at home all day long.
B) Visit the amazing national park nearby.
C) Create a lot of problems when in school.
D) Take walks with his family close to home.

2
A) His time commitment to the natural environment.
B) The black and white photographs that he took of nature.
C) The exact photocopy images of the national park in his pictures.
D) The books he wrote about the technical aspects of taking pictures.

3
A) He wanted to show his love for nature.
B) He didn't want humans to build highways.
C) He wanted to remember his father's teaching.
D) He wanted humans and nature to live in peace.

UNIT 8

Companions or test subjects?

Warm-up

Directions: You will listen to a conversation between a man and a woman about adopting a laboratory dog. After listening, complete the exercises in "What did you hear?" and "How would you respond?"

1 What did you hear?

Decide whether the following statements are true (T) or false (F) according to what you have heard.

1) (T/F) The woman wanted a dog that wasn't used for testing at first.

2) (T/F) The scientists wouldn't permit the tested dogs to be adopted.

3) (T/F) The tested dogs were quite friendly but looked funny or damaged.

4) (T/F) The woman decided to give one of these tested dogs a better life in the end.

2 How would you respond?

Please give your personal opinions by choosing one of the answers in the following two questions.

1) Would you like to adopt a dog that was tested?
   A) Yes.
   B) No.
   C) Probably.

2) Do you think animals have the right to live a better life?
   A) Yes.
   B) No.
   C) Probably.

Listening

Understanding a conversation

Directions: Listen to a conversation and choose the best answer from the four choices provided for each question.

The following questions are based on what you have just heard.

1
A) Because she is too sensitive to wild animals.
B) Because animals are equals to human beings.
C) Because animals are losing humans' support.
D) Because animals need protection from humans.

2
A) They should test drugs and sprays on animals.
B) They should test drugs and sprays on humans.
C) They should not do horrible things to animals.
D) They should stop using drugs in their lab tests.

3
A) Scientific technology has made animals suffer less.
B) There's less need to test animals for medical reasons.
C) Animals shouldn't suffer for every medical product.
D) Drugs would've been dangerous without animal tests.

4
A) They should be destroyed right after they are tested.
B) They should be sent to a quiet place to end their lives.
C) They deserve the right to get help from organisations.
D) They deserve better treatment for their help to humans.

Understanding a passage

Directions: Listen to a passage and choose the best answer from the four choices provided for each question.

The following questions are based on what you have just heard.

1
A) They found out where to get clean energy sources.
B) They flew around the world in the *Solar Impulse 2*.
C) They designed an airplane that doesn't need energy for power.
D) They designed a solar-powered plane that can travel a long distance.

2
A) It was the first flight around the world with two pilots.
B) It has wings that are much smaller than other airplanes.
C) It flew the longest distance for any sun-powered airplane.
D) It finished the journey and flew back earlier than planned.

3
A) It is as large as a passenger airplane.
B) It enables pilots to fly six days without stopping.
C) It doesn't require pilots to wear an oxygen mask.
D) It can be powered for a very long time even at night.

4
A) The journey back to Hawaii turned out harder.
B) The batteries of the airplane became damaged.
C) It had a big and unexpected trouble with its engine.
D) It couldn't land at the same place in the Middle East.

Speaking

Practicing conversational skills

Useful expressions: Expressing emotional feelings

I feel comfortable around him.
I feel happy about his promotion.
I feel very sad about his family tragedy.
I feel angry at his rudeness and improper behavior.

I was shocked to hear they got married.
I was stunned to see such amazing architecture.
I was so disappointed to learn about the bad news.
I was excited to find out about the new study-abroad program.

I feel depressed that the boss gave me so much work.
I feel confident that the project will be accomplished soon.
I feel so upset that our proposal was rejected by the committee.
I feel hopeful that students can get financial aid starting next month.

Model dialogues

Dialogue 1

A: You look depressed. What happened?
B: I have felt so bad the whole day today.
A: Really? Anything I can do to help?
B: Guess no one can help. Melissa broke up with me.
A: Oh, poor you! I'm shocked to hear that.
B: You know this made me so upset.
A: But a bad mood will only make things worse.
B: Then what would you do if you were in my shoes?

A: Well, if I were you, I would just let it go.
B: I wish I could, but I feel so depressed now.
A: Come on. Just take it easy and listen to music.
B: Does that work?
A: Believe me it works because I often do that when I feel bad.
B: OK. I'll take your advice and try to change my mood.

Dialogue 2

A: Linda, do you have some time for me?
B: Sure. You look unhappy. What's wrong?
A: I just feel confused about the people around me.
B: Oh? Interesting! For example?
A: My friends like you are all very nice and considerate.
B: That's what friends are for.
A: However, my boss is always inconsiderate!
B: Why don't you talk to your boss?
A: I did, but nothing has changed.
B: Well, don't worry about it. It's probably no big deal.
A: I know, but he never cares how I feel.
B: So what? He's your boss, not your friend. Anyhow, I believe your boss will see your value later.
A: Hope so. I feel a little better now. Thanks, Linda.
B: My pleasure. Hope you feel happier.

Now, it's your turn!

Situational dialogue 1

"You're very happy and excited about your recent date with someone. You met him/her at a party and you both fell in love at first sight. You can't help but share your emotional feelings with your best friend."

Situational dialogue 2

"Your friend failed the English oral test, so he/she feels very upset and depressed. He/she dared not to tell his/her parents nor did he/she want to let his/her classmates know about it. However, since you're his/her best friend, he/she is telling you about the test result and how he/she feels now."

Listening and speaking: Conversation

Task 1 Based on what you have heard from the conversation, answer the following two questions by filling in the blanks with proper words or phrases.

1) What's so special about this national park in California?
The national park is full of beautiful ______________, and they are called ______________.

2) Why are the trees in this national park so special?
They're __________ in size and the ______________ in the world. They're also very __________.

Task 2 Now listen to the conversation again. After listening, please complete the following chart to illustrate why these redwood trees can grow so tall and live so long.

Reason	Explanation
These trees live in healthy soil.	The soil contains rich acid.
The weather is __________ for them.	The trees get ______________ from the ocean.
They're also naturally very __________.	The trees don't suffer from ______________.
These trees can ______________.	The outside covering of the trees is very __________.

Speak out!

"If you had been to Huangshan or any well-known mountains in China, you would surely be stunned by their spectacular scenery. However, the beautiful scenery has been threatened by humans, just like the redwood trees in the national park in California. To stop humans' irresponsible damage to the natural environment, you're now engaged in a problem-solving activity with your group members by listing "do's" and "don'ts" on a sheet of paper."

Listening and speaking: Passage

Task 1 Complete the chart by filling in the boxes with the people provided below according to their opinions stated on the right.

The speaker | Medical scientists | The general public | Animal rights activists

People	Opinion
Mahatma Ghandi	The greatness of a nation and its moral progress can be judged by the way its animals are treated.
	It's cruel to make animals suffer to benefit humans because an animal's life is just as important as a person's life.
	Medical advances wouldn't be possible without animal testing. Any suffering that animals experience is necessary to help humans.
	Humans shouldn't have bad intentions to harm animals, and we should treat animals like we treat humans.
	Animals have been gaining more rights in recent years, so there may soon be some changes in the way humans use animals.

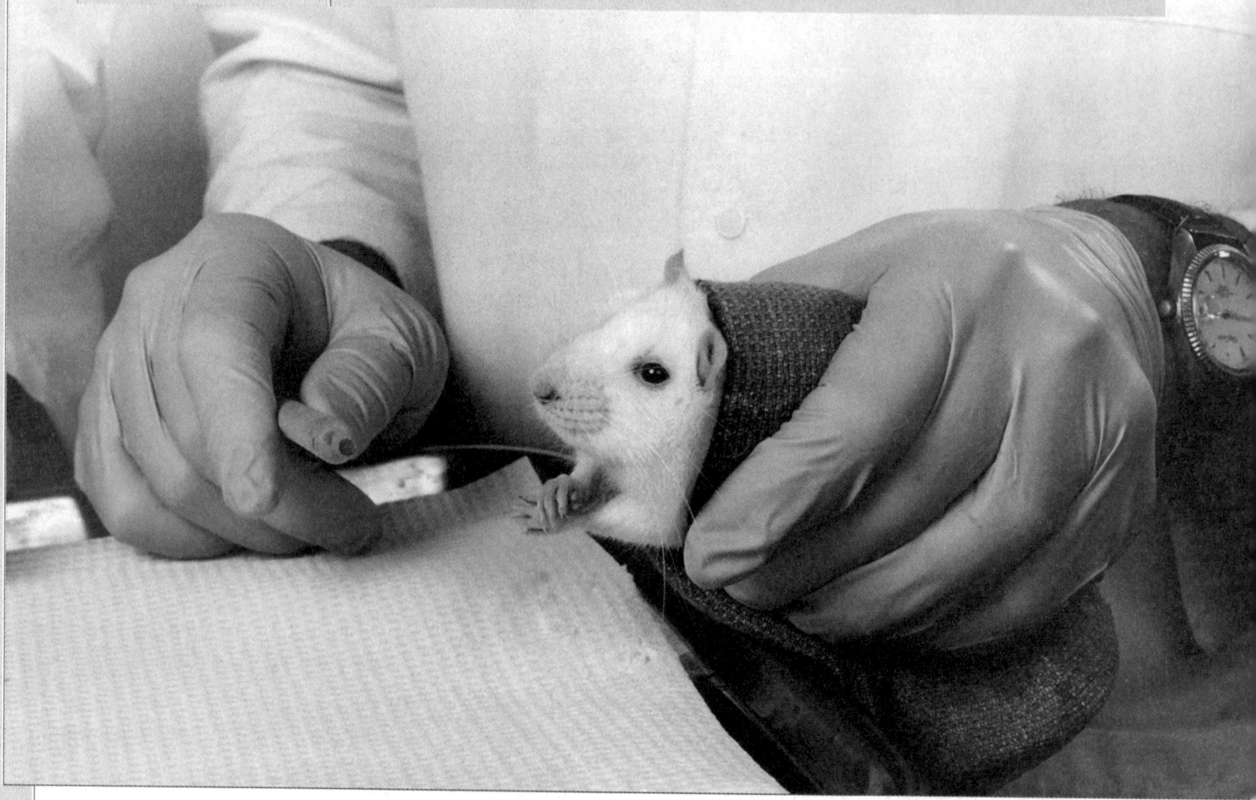

Task 2 Now listen to the passage again. After listening, match the left column with the right based on the information you have heard. Put appropriate letters next to the numbers.

Why	Reason
____ 1) The activists are very upset.	a They are in a cage with no opportunity to be outside.
____ 2) Lab animals live a terrible life.	b These animals never receive kindness and affection.
____ 3) It's cruel to make animals suffer.	c Each side has a strong passion for their beliefs.
____ 4) This debate won't disappear.	d An animal's life is as important as a person's life.

Speak out!

“You are now being engaged in a team debate on this topic: Who is to blame for the dangerous medicines given to pregnant women in the incident? The doctors who allow pregnant women to take untested drugs or the activists who strongly oppose using animals for medical tests?”

UNIT REPORT

You're required to prepare a two-minute speech on one of the following topics or any topic related to the unit theme. You will be asked to present it in the next class.

- Love me, love my dog
- Why we shouldn't use lab animals
- Human health is more important than animal rights

Sample:

Hello, everyone. Every time when I saw people walking dogs on the streets, I would ask myself a question, "Do animals deserve the right to live a good life?" Yes, the answer is clear and firm. However, my second question would be, "Are they as important as humans or should they enjoy equal rights as humans?" Then I would hesitate and choose the word "No". Why not? To me, the newborn babies, the elderly, and many others weigh much more than animals on my scale. Don't be mistaken, I don't mean animals are not important, but if I have to choose one of them, I would have to choose people. Animals, in my opinion, should be secondary to humans. Thanks for letting me share with you my personal opinion.

Homework

Section A: Understanding news reports

News report 1

Directions: Now you will hear a news report. At the end of the report, you will hear some questions. After you hear a question, choose the best answer from the four choices.

The following questions are based on what you have just heard.

1
A) They return to their own country.
B) They head to the Olympic Games.
C) They advertise for big companies.
D) They accept a large sum of money.

2
A) Indonesia.
B) The United States.
C) Singapore.
D) Sweden.

3
A) To sell their Olympic medals.
B) To compete for a wealthy country.
C) To advertise products for small companies.
D) To advertise products for large companies.

News report 2

Directions: Now you will hear a news report. At the end of the report, you will hear some questions. After you hear a question, choose the best answer from the four choices.

The following questions are based on what you have just heard.

1

A) To catch a large, elegant, white swan in a river.
B) To go up and down the river to check the boats.
C) To count the men in boats who wear red jackets.
D) To count the swans that swim in a river in London.

2

A) They want to catch the swans to eat them.
B) They want to give the swans a health check.
C) They want to send the swans to royal families.
D) They want to follow an English old tradition.

Section B: Understanding passages

Directions: Now you will hear a passage. At the end of the passage, you will hear some questions. After you hear a question, choose the best answer from the four choices.

The following questions are based on what you have just heard.

1
A) Because their treatment made his health a little better.
B) Because the different drugs that he tried were effective.
C) Because he had many years of suffering from breathing.
D) Because he didn't smoke and lived in a good environment.

2
A) He could breathe much better than before.
B) His breathing problem became worse again.
C) He stopped the treatment by confused doctors.
D) He died mysteriously right after he came back.

3
A) Through investigating his trip to Australia.
B) Through studying his body after his death.
C) Through reviewing other aspects of his life.
D) Through watching his musical performance.

4
A) He cleaned his musical instrument too frequently.
B) His lungs were infected while travelling in Australia.
C) He played an instrument only good for Scottish people.
D) He played an instrument that had a dangerous substance.

U校园智慧教学云平台使用指南

亲爱的同学，你好！欢迎使用U校园智慧教学云平台（以下简称“U校园”）。

U校园为高校外语教学提供教、学、评、测、研一站式混合教学解决方案，**通过优质的学习内容、高效的教学工具、互通的多终端支持**，全方位提升学习体验和教学效果。

数字课程使用指南

本教材提供两门数字课程：教材配套课程和U卡通课程，均基于U校园使用。

教材配套课程提供与教材相对应的学习内容与管理功能，可支持自主学习、师生互动、班级管理与在线测评等，有助于提升学习效率与教学质量。

U卡通课程提供更多样的学习资源，包括语言技能培养、文化素养提升、商务职场拓展等数字课程，以及大学英语四、六级备考训练资源等，可供院校根据需要选择使用，作为教材的有益拓展，满足外语教学与学习的个性化需求。

使用步骤

Step 1 使用电脑打开U校园首页（u.unipus.cn），完成注册，登录系统；也可使用手机在应用市场下载“U校园学生版”App或扫描右侧二维码下载，完成注册，登录系统。

Step 2 登录后，选择你所在的学校，输入你的学号和姓名，完成身份认证。

如认证不成功，可能是因为贵校尚未开通U校园或导入学生名单，请联系授课教师，以学校为单位联系外研社市场经理开通或导入。

Step 3 选择对应级别的教材配套课程并使用书后验证码激活。验证码提供两种形式：18位字符和二维码，信息一致，效用相同，使用一种形式激活课程后，另一种即时失效。可选择在电脑端或手机端输入18位字符，或使用手机端扫描二维码激活课程。课程激活后在电脑端和手机端均可使用。

教材配套课程验证码可在U校园和外研随身学App分别激活，请注意保管。

Step 4 选择U卡通课程并使用书后验证码激活。验证码提供两种形式：18位字符和二维码，信息一致，效用相同，使用一种形式激活课程后，另一种即时失效。可选择在电脑端或手机端输入18位字符，或使用手机端扫描二维码激活课程。课程激活后在电脑端和手机端均可使用。

U卡通课程由校方统一选定，激活前请向授课教师咨询贵校是否有统一的课程选择安排，以免选错课程造成损失。

外研随身学App使用指南

为方便同学利用碎片化时间进行外语学习，本教材还特别提供外研随身学App，听课文、看视频、学单词、练口语，随时随地，想学就学。

使用步骤

Step 1 使用手机在应用市场下载“外研随身学”App或扫描右侧二维码下载，完成注册，登录系统。

Step 2 选择对应课程并使用书后验证码激活。验证码提供两种形式：18位字符和二维码，信息一致，效用相同，使用一种形式激活课程后，另一种即时失效。可选择输入18位字符或扫描二维码激活课程。

教材配套课程验证码可在U校园和外研随身学App分别激活，请注意保管。

注意事项

1. 书后贴有两个验证码，分别对应激活教材配套课程及U卡通课程，请注意查看和区分。
2. 验证码可在自教材印刷日期起两年内激活，逾期未使用将被视为放弃。
3. 每个验证码在U校园和外研随身学App只能分别使用一次，激活成功后自动失效。
4. 激活成功后，教材配套课程使用有效期为1年，U卡通课程使用有效期为6个月。
5. 验证码不记名、不挂失、不可转让、不可退换、遗失不补，请妥善保管。
6. 外语教学与研究出版社及北京外研在线数字科技有限公司对验证码使用有最终解释权。

常见问题

ⓘ 我的验证码为什么不能激活课程？

请先排除以下情况：

A. 输错验证码；

B. 输入的验证码与选择的数字课程名称不匹配；

C. 验证码已被其他人使用过。

如以上情况均不存在，请咨询客服。

ⓘ 我的验证码在U校园激活过了，为什么外研随身学App上的课程还不能使用？

需要分别在U校园和外研随身学App对课程进行激活，每个平台都需要单独激活课程后才能使用，且请确保在两个平台激活时使用的是同一个账号，否则无法激活。

ⓘ 我的验证码还没有使用就丢失或损坏了怎么办？

书后验证码提供两种形式：18位字符和二维码，信息一致，效用相同。验证码遗失不补，请一定妥善保管。若丢失需通过正规渠道购买新教材。若18位字符损坏，可扫描二维码激活课程。若二维码损坏，可选择输入18位字符激活课程。

ⓘ 我能把我的账号和密码给我的同学使用吗？

不能。教师需要通过账号查询你的学习进度和答题情况并进行评估，如果和其他同学混用账号，教师将无法对你的学习情况进行客观评价。

ⓘ 登录U校园后，为什么没有看到我要学习的课程？

请确认是否发生以下情况：

A. 学校管理员未分配班课。请联系授课教师确认课程是否分配。

B. 加错班级。可退出错误班级，联系授课教师获得正确的班课邀请码，重新加班。

ⓘ U校园App与外研随身学App有何不同？

U校园App是U校园平台移动端，内容全面，包括教材内容与补充练习及资源；由学校统一开通，按教学班级使用，分学生版和教师版，有教学管理功能。外研随身学App主要供学生自学，提供教材中适合碎片化学习的部分，如课文录音、课程视频等；由学生自主注册使用，无教师版和教学管理功能。

ⓘ 为什么U校园App/外研随身学App中的音视频内容无法播放？

未下载的音视频内容，请确保在网络畅通的环境下进行播放；已下载的音视频内容，如无法播放，请尝试重新下载，或者咨询客服。

ⓘ 如何下载和删除U校园App/外研随身学App中的音视频文件？

下载：点击每单元目录页右上角的下载按钮，可下载本单元所有的音视频文件。

删除：在“我的”→“设置”中选择“清除缓存”，可清除已下载的音视频文件。

ⓘ 是否可以导出U校园App/外研随身学App中已下载的音视频文件？

音视频文件只支持App内下载和播放，不支持导出。

客服邮箱：service@unipus.cn
客服电话：400 898 7008
客服QQ：4008987008

该QQ账号为Unipus官方企业号，
添加前请务必仔细核查。